BURT FRANKLIN: RESEARCH & SOURCE WORKS SERIES 882
Philosophy Monograph Series 87

FRAGMENTS

ON ETHICAL SUBJECTS

FRAGMENTS

ON ETHICAL SUBJECTS

BY THE LATE

GEORGE GROTE, F.R.S.

BEING

A SELECTION FROM HIS POSTHUMOUS PAPERS

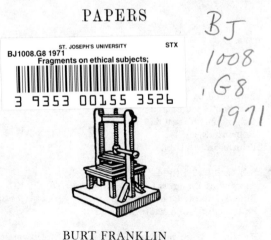

BURT FRANKLIN
NEW YORK

Published by LENOX HILL Pub. & Dist. Co. (Burt Franklin)
235 East 44th St., New York, N.Y. 10017
Originally Published: 1876
Reprinted: 1971
Printed in the U.S.A.

S.B.N.: 8337-14694
Library of Congress Card Catalog No.: 78-179391
Burt Franklin: Research and Source Works Series 882
Philosophy Monograph Series 87

Reprinted from the original edition in the University of Illinois
at Urbana, Library.

INTRODUCTION.

WHEN Mr. Grote's vast collection of MSS. came to be thoroughly examined, there were discovered several Essays in Ethics, which appeared to be sufficiently consecutive and complete to be given to the world.

The work on Plato afforded him opportunities for discussing various points of Ethical theory; and he turned these opportunities to good account: but in none of his published writings had he treated systematically of the questions relating to Morals, in the form that they usually assume in the treatises of modern writers.

Ethical Philosophy formed, all through life, one of his chief lines of study. He had followed its development, both as to its theoretical foundations and as to its practical or preceptive details, in ancient and in modern times. His own views may possibly have been shaped by his early contact with James Mill; but they were matured by his own independent meditations. Mr. Grote belonged to the Utilitarian school; and in the statement of the doctrines, as well as in the arguments used, there is much that is common to all its disciples; yet his superior erudition, together with his great powers both as a reasoner and as a writer, impart a welcome freshness to his handling of the subject in these papers.

The first Essay—On the Origin and Nature of Ethical Sentiment—raises the Psychological question of Ethics, the mental foundations of the sentiment of right and wrong. After giving the elements that enter into the sentiment, he defines it generally as a sentiment of regulated social reciprocity, as between the agent and the society wherein he lives. This is the *Form*, which it presents in every grade of its development. There are also in the *Matter*, some points of capital uniformity, which he enumerates; but account has also to be taken of the original and inherent diversities between one age or country and another. He urges strongly the bearing of this fact on the theory of an Instinctive Moral Sentiment; and meets the objection, urged against the derivation theory, that it tends to weaken the authority of the ethical motive.

The second Essay — Philosophy of Morals — is a short discussion of the Moral Standard. The author takes his ground upon the juridical view of Morality, brought into prominence by Bentham and Austin, and illustrates it with great force. He enquires into the meaning of the "supremacy of conscience," and connects it, under all its disguises, with a reference to external authority. He re-urges the essential *reciprocity* of obligation and right, and criticises Kant's theory of the moral feelings.

The third Essay — Ancient Systems of Moral Philosophy—goes no farther than to advert to the defectiveness of the ancient systems in making their starting-point the *summum bonum*, or the happiness of the individual. The real end of morality being, not to make the individual happy, but to protect one man from another man, the theory of the *summum bonum* had to be stretched and interpreted to contain a reference to the welfare of others. The author shews that the adherence to this starting-point was the cause of much of the perplexity and confusion of ideas that we find in the ancient moralists ; not even excepting Aristotle himself.

The fourth Essay—Idea of Ethical Philosophy —is the fullest in its handling of the several topics brought forward. The author repeats the social bearings of Obligation, viewing society as the immediate source of the ethical sanction; but indicates that there is a farther enquiry—on what does Society itself proceed in framing its enactments? and this conducts to the question of how far utility or happiness is the ultimate end.

The second part of the Essay is occupied with tracing at some length the growth of ethical ideas in the child; while, in the third part, the author goes fully into the nature and meanings of Moral Approbation and Moral Disapprobation.

The two concluding Essays, had they been discovered in time, would have been included in the 'Aristotle.' They are the fruit of long and laborious study, and, so far as they extend, embody the writer's matured views upon the Ethics and the Politics: the two treatises whose omission from his published exposition of the Aristotelian philosophy has been most regretted.

The fifth Essay—On the Ethics of Aristotle— falls naturally into two divisions: the first treats of Happiness; the second of what, according to Aristotle, is the chief ingredient of Happiness, namely, Virtue. On Aristotle's own conception of

Happiness, Mr. Grote dwells very minutely; turning it over on all sides, and looking at it from every point of view. While fully acknowledging its merits, he gives also the full measure of its defects. His criticisms on this head are in the author's best style, and are no less important as regards Ethical discussion · than as a commentary on Aristotle.

His handling of Aristotle's doctrine of Virtue is equally subtle and instructive. Particularly striking are the remarks on the *Voluntary* and the *Involuntary*, and on προαίρεσις, or *deliberate preference*. The treatment of the Virtues in detail is, unhappily, more fragmentary; but what he does say regarding Justice and Equity has a permanent interest.

The concluding Essay—The Politics of Aristotle —must be studied in connection with the preceding. Although but a brief sketch, it is remarkable for the insight which it affords us into the most consummate political Ideal of the ancient world.

A. B.

CONTENTS.

ESSAY I.

ON THE ORIGIN AND NATURE OF ETHICAL SENTIMENT.

ON THE ORIGIN AND NATURE OF ETHICAL SENTIMENT.

OF all the remaining productions of the ancient world, there is nothing which is more characteristic and admirable than the writings of the Greek and Roman philosophers on the subject of ethical and political science. By them these sciences were first created, not only without any particular facilities for the attempt, but in spite of a very narrow range of experience and observation—in spite of entire want of intercourse with all nations not Hellenic—and, what is of still greater moment, without any pre-existing specimens of philosophical enquiry on that or any other subject to serve them either as model or incentive.

To understand clearly what the Greek and Roman writers achieved in this department of human knowledge, two preliminary explanations are necessary.

1. To give a general view of that which constitutes ethical sentiment, and the sources from whence it derives its origin.

2. To present an account of the state of ethical

sentiment as it stood in the Hellenic world prior to Socrates, with whom the day-star of philosophical enquiries on ethical subjects may be considered to have arisen.

What is Ethical Sentiment?

The explanations given by different writers of the nature and origin of ethical sentiment have been many and various; but every one who has ever either spoken or written upon the subject has agreed in considering this sentiment as absolutely indispensable to the very existence of society. Without the diffusion of a certain measure of this feeling throughout all the members of the social union, the caprice, the desires, and the passions of each separate individual would render the maintenance of any established communion impossible. Positive morality, under some form or another, has existed in every society of which the world has ever had experience.

But if we compare one age with another, and one part of the globe with another, the differences in respect to ethical sentiment will appear both vastly numerous and prodigiously important. Some few leading points of similarity will be found to prevail always and everywhere; but the points of difference will be found to outnumber greatly those in regard

to which an uniformity of sentiment reigns throughout all the various communities of the world.   Any
theory which professes to explain the origin and
nature of ethical sentiment must render an account,
not merely of the points of resemblance, but also of
the many and great divergences between one society
and another.

No theory can satisfy this condition which repre-
sents ethical sentiment as consisting of inexplicable
instincts, or mental determinations originally arising
without any regard to consequences.   Those who
adopt this view of the case produce the supposed
instincts for the purpose of explaining those modifications of ethical sentiment which are the most
common and universal—they do not imagine special
instincts in this or that age or nation to explain
what is separate and peculiar.   Yet if the theory of
instinct be applied to the former, consistency im-
periously requires that it shall be applied to the
latter ; the more so as the latter includes all that is
really or intrinsically difficult of explanation.   For
the former, or the universal and essential tendencies
of the moral sense, admit of being most satisfactorily
deduced from other elementary principles of our
nature.

Ethical sentiment is, in fact, a very complicated
sentiment, presupposing many trains of ideas and
feelings, and deduced from several distinct, and even

opposing elements of our nature; yet so combined together by habitual association, as to affect the mind with the rapidity and instantaneousness of a simple feeling, no separate consciousness of the constituent items remaining.

The elementary tendencies of the mind which ethical sentiment presupposes, and out of which it is more or less deduced, are as follows :—

1. *Our self-regarding tendencies.*

The whole of every man's comfort and happiness, from the cradle to the tomb, depends upon the forbearance, the protection, and the positive help of others; and all these consequences, again, depend upon the dispositions which others entertain towards him. This dependence is great and complete throughout the whole of life; but is most urgently felt during the utter helplessness of childhood, at the time when the first associations are formed.

2. *Our sympathetic tendencies.*

Generally speaking, and leaving out of sight particular cases of exception, the pains of others are an original cause of pain to ourselves. Several exceptions might be enumerated to this rule, such as the " Suave mari magno," of Lucretius; but the rule in general holds good.

The pleasures of others are frequently a cause of pleasure to ourselves, but by no means universally.

The exceptions in this case are very frequent and numerous.

But the sympathy of others, either with our pains or with our pleasures, is always agreeable to us: want of sympathy on the part of others, or the manifestation of a feeling the opposite of sympathy, is always painful and disagreeable.

3. *Our benevolent affections.*

We love those who confer happiness upon us, or protect us from suffering : we also love those whose presence is associated with our enjoyments, or with our consciousness of protection.

4. *Our malevolent affections.*

We hate those who are the causes of suffering to us, or who deprive us of happiness either present or expected ; also those whose presence is associated with suffering or loss of enjoyment.

5. Sympathising with other persons who feel pain, we are disposed to hate those who are the causes of that pain, though not with the same intensity as we hate those who are the causes of pain to ourselves. Sympathising with others who feel pleasure, we are disposed to love those who are the causes of that pleasure.

Amongst all these different affections, the self-regarding affections are both the strongest, the most constant, and the most lasting. The sympathetic and the benevolent affections are capable of becoming frequent and powerful causes of action under a good training, as the malevolent affections often do under an opposite system. It seems to be by virtue of the benevolent and sympathetic affections acting conjointly with the self-regarding affections, that we become capable of conceiving intense attachment to a common good—that is, to the idea of the safety and happiness of others in conjunction with our own —and apprehensions equally intense at the idea of a common peril or suffering.

Every individual person is placed in a double position in respect to his conduct and sentiments. In the first place, he is an *agent*, seeking to satisfy various wants, and to gratify various affections in the easiest manner open to him. In this character, his interests and his feelings stand apart from those of other persons, not unfrequently at variance with them. In the second place, he is a *patient*, in common with others, from the action of different individuals: in this character his interests and his feelings are commonly in unison with those of others. Throughout the whole of life he is constantly placed in both of these two positions, and he accordingly acquires the constant habit of viewing and judging of the circumstances around him both from the one point of view and from the other. When he is about to become an agent, he unconsciously passes from the point of view belonging to this character to place himself by imagination in that of the spectator or patient; when he is witness to the agency of others, his fancy transfers him to the position of the agent, and presents to him a conception of the state of mind which would animate him if he himself were so placed. The habit of thus changing our point of view, and conceiving what we should feel if placed in a position different from our own, is necessarily an acquired habit; but it is acquired so early, it is so constantly called into exercise, and is so indispensably necessary at all times to our comfort and even our safety, that it becomes at last one of the most rapid and familiar of all the mental processes. We come to perform it not only without any distinct or special consciousness, but also in cases where it causes us extreme pain, and where we would greatly desire to escape it. The idea of the judgment which others will form becomes constantly and indissolubly associated with the idea of action in the mind of every agent ; this idea being, in fact, the same (with some differences which shall be touched upon presently) as the idea of that judgment which he himself would form if placed in the position of others. It is, in fact, the idea of the judgment of others, concurrently with his own as a spectator or patient.

This idea of the judgment of others upon our conduct and feelings as agents, or the idea of our own judgment as spectators in concurrence with others, upon our own conduct as agents, is the main basis. of what is properly called *ethical sentiment*; which is essentially a social sentiment, conceivable only by a number of men living in some sort of communion more or less intimate and extensive.

Ethical sentiment is by no means identical either with sympathy or with the benevolent affection, although it is a compound which presupposes both the one and the other. A man may feel both sympathy and benevolence in the most acute degree towards a being who cannot be an object of ethical sentiment—towards an infant, an idiot, or an animal; he may be powerfully restrained by ethical sentiment in his dealings with a person towards whom he indulges little or no benevolence, or whom he even regards as a personal enemy. Ethical sentiment is an aggregate of the opinions entertained by each given community, and associated in their minds with very strong feelings—as to the line of conduct which entitles any individual agent to their protection, their esteem, or their admiration on the one hand—or which exposes him on the other hand to their displeasure, their contempt, or their indifference. It consists of an association in my mind of a certain line of conduct, on the part both of myself and of any other individual agent, with a certain sentiment resulting from such conduct, and excited by it, in the minds of the general public around us. It is a sentiment of *regulated social reciprocity*, as between the agent and the society amongst whom he lives—such and such behaviour to be rendered on his part, such and such sentiments to be manifested as requital on theirs. It is the opinion which he entertains, and which has been deeply impressed upon his mind by its connection with his most anxious hopes and fears, on the conditions prescribed to him for obtaining, first the protection, next the esteem, and lastly the admiration of the society—and for escaping the distress and misery consequent upon his becoming, or even upon his conceiving himself to be, the object of their anger, or scorn, or displeasure. All ethical sentiment, of what kind soever it be, whether perfect or imperfect, well or ill directed, uniformly contains these three ingredients :—1. The idea of a certain conduct or disposition on the part of each individual agent. 2. The idea of a certain disposition or conduct on the part of other persons towards such agent, determined by his conduct and disposition as it may have been manifested, or as there may be reason to understand it. These two ideas, intimately combined and blended together by association, conceived (3), as bound together by a common sanction, and as reciprocating one with the other, seem to constitute all that is universal, essential, and indispensable to ethical sentiment, taken as it exists in its lowest and most perverted, as well as in its purest and most correct, varieties. The *reciprocity* between the agent and the society consists in this, that although he does not expect to receive the protection or favour of society, except upon condition of certain conduct and certain dispositions on his part, failing which, he anticipates from them the contrary treatment—yet, on the other hand, if he *has* duly performed these conditions, he conceives himself to have earned their protection or favour as a matter of right, and thinks that they would do him wrong if they withheld it.

I say, moreover, *these two ideas conceived as bound together by a common sanction.* To a certain extent the sanction thus implied in our moral sentiment is actually exhibited in the positive interference and in the manifestation of sentiment on the part of society. In most cases, the various acts and forbearances which a man supposes to constitute the sum of his duty, especially in a rude stage of civilization, are acts and forbearances towards other individuals: and here, the body of the society forms the positive sanction on which a man relies for interference and protection, when he feels that he has performed the conditions which give him a title to claim it. If the social organization be so imperfect as to disappoint his hopes of such protection— or if the persons against whom he requires protection should themselves chance to be the most powerful portion of society—the agent thus disappointed looks to the Gods as a supplementary sanction. The idea of a *sanction*, or of a superior force competent to interfere and prepared to interfere as a guarantee for the maintenance of the connection between the two ideas above alluded to, forms a constant adjunct of ethical sentiment—however imperfectly the reality may correspond to this imagination. The intimate connection established in the mind by association between good or ill desert and its consequences, drives us to conceive an ideal *vinculum* between them, under the form of a superintending and ever-watchful Providence, competent to punish, to compensate, and to reward.

These, then, are the constituent elements of ethical sentiment, which it includes universally and under all circumstances—the idea of certain acts and forbearances, manifesting particular dispositions, on the part of any given agent, considered as the exciting cause of those dispositions on the part of others upon which the safety and happiness of the agent most vitally depend—of their protection or ill-usage, their admiration or scorn, their esteem or neglect. Association knits together the two intimately and indissolubly in the mind of the agent—the idea of the act or disposition on his own part with that of the corresponding disposition on the part of others—in-such manner that the one cannot be thought of without the other, and a compound sentiment is formed, the items of which cannot become subjects of distinct consciousness.   As a cement and guarantee to the constancy of this union, the idea of an extraneous sanction is superadded, and completes what may be called the *Form* of Ethical Sentiment, as distinguished from the *Matter*.

In regard to the *Matter* of Ethical Sentiment, there is in some few capital points a great uniformity; but there are also, upon almost all other points, the widest divergencies, between different ages and different nations.   First, Ethical Sentiment always places some limit upon the malevolent dispositions of mankind, and upon the indefinite power which each man originally possesses of hurting or tormenting his neighbours.   In the very rudest communities, some limitation of this kind is imposed by the general sentiment; without it, indeed, no community whatever could even continue to exist.   The association is everywhere more or less formed, in the mind of each individual agent, between acts of intentional hurt or spoliation of others, and the displeasure or enmity of society.   Every member of the society feels this sentiment with greater or less force : every one finds and feels his own protection in it.   There are great differences between one society and another in respect to the faintness or potency of the feeling—

the constancy or unsteadiness of its operation—the degree to which it bears equally or unequally upon all the various members, and operates alike for the protection of all and the restraint of all. But all societies agree, so far as the existence of the feeling is concerned, in this portion of the *matter* of ethical sentiment, and it forms the indispensable link which enables them to subsist and move on without dissolution. The coincidence of interest, or indeed of necessity, between one society and another, is in this particular so evidently and urgently impressed, that it would be astonishing if the effects produced were not uniform.

Again, ethical sentiment tends universally, under all its forms and varieties, to develop and encourage the benevolent impulses of our nature. It produces this effect in some communities to a greater degree, in other communities to a less degree: but in all, without exception, it produces an effect in this direction. In the first place, the restraint, before alluded to, which it imposes upon the malevolent and rapacious propensities of our nature, is indispensably necessary to make room for any considerable growth and development of the benevolent impulses. A man who is perpetually in fear of evil at the hands of others is hardly susceptible of a decided or constant feeling of benevolence towards them: it is only when he ceases to be beset with the former feeling that the latter association acquires any forcible hold of his mind. In the next place, over and above the indirect encouragement, thus afforded by clearing the ground from obstructive and antagonizing feelings, ethical sentiment affords further positive encouragement to the benevolent impulses. The voice of society is everywhere more or less favourable to them, even in the least civilized tribes recorded in history.

Thirdly, ethical sentiment is also the great generator and supporter of all the virtues included under the general term of self-command, including prudence, temperance, courage, continence, repression of anger, &c. The constant habit in the agent, of making present to himself the judgment of the public, is the grand and effectual curb by which his selfish and impetuous appetites are kept in reasonable subjection.

Ethical sentiment, therefore, when viewed with reference not to its *Form*, but to its *Matter*, exhibits a certain general similarity of direction in all times and places. It tends uniformly and everywhere, in a greater or less degree, to place some limit on individual malevolence and cupidity; to foster the benevolent impulses of our nature; to encourage the habit of individual self-command; and to implant the notion of a certain recognised standard of action, for the adjustment of each man's behaviour.

But when this uniformity of general direction has once been stated, we cannot with truth carry the analogy any farther. In no two countries and in no two ages is this general effect produced, either to the same degree or in the same manner. If we make a list of the various actions reputed *guilty, disgraceful, wrong*, or *unbecoming*, or conversely, of actions *virtuous, honourable, right*, or *becoming*, in any given age or country,—we shall find that our list will be altogether inapplicable if we try it with reference to any distant region or anterior stage of society. The virtuous man or the vicious man, of our own age or country, will no longer receive the same denominations if transferred to a remote climate or a different people. Though the same terms of praise and blame are employed, it will be found that in one society they are directed towards one class of actions, in another society towards another. If we compare the positive morality of Japan, of Hindostan, of Turkey, of England, of Brazil, of the American Indians, of the ancient Greeks, Romans, and Germans, we shall perceive that amongst any one of these nations a man might be exposed to the abhorrence of society for actions which amongst the rest of them would be perfectly innocent. There exist amongst each of them, peculiar errors, superstitions, antipathies, and caprices, handed down and cherished as an integral portion of the national ethical sentiment, quite as much reverenced as that other portion which the nation holds in common with others,—in many cases, indeed, much more reverenced. When we consider ethical sentiment with reference, not to its *Form*, but to its *Matter*, we cannot but discern that the uniformity and similarity, as between various societies, does not extend beyond a few capital points, of obvious and pressing necessity, and in addition to this, a general analogy of aim and direction. The rest is all peculiarity and diversity: on which each age and each nation clings to tenets of its own, without recognising any basis of reference common to itself with others.

And it is obvious that such peculiarities would naturally arise, amongst different societies all rude and ignorant, in those early processes of association out of which ethical sentiment is first constituted. To love the causes of their security and happiness— to hate the causes of their perils and misery—are universal currents of the principle of association, which each of these rude societies would obey on its own ground—the signs and concomitants of either of these important results would also share in the feeling more specially belonging to the cause. In so far, then, as the causes of happiness or misery were obvious, immediate, not to be overlooked or mistaken,— these communities would all form the like judgments and attach the like ethical sentiments. But in such a rude condition of the human intellect, mistakes as to the real causes of happiness and misery would be innumerable, and each society would make a different mistake : moreover, among the different signs and concomitants, accident would turn the attention of each society upon some in preference to the rest. Differences would hence arise, in the original constitution of ethical sentiment, as conceived by each community : and such peculiarities, when once conceived and incorporated with the general body of ethical sentiment, would be transmitted from generation to generation, by the omnipotence of early habit and training—they would be inseparable and incorrigible, except by some greater improvement than history has ever yet recorded. There would be as much caprice and peculiarity, in the various divergences of ethical sentiment, as there is in the choice of particular phenomena as omens and signs of the future.

In treating of the origin and authority of our moral sentiment, many writers have paid more attention to the *Matter* of this sentiment than to the *Form*, and have considered the latter as if it were something subordinate to and dependent upon the former. The idea or the sight of certain actions (they say), without any regard to their consequences, excites in our minds a certain simple and inexplicable feeling, called ethical approbation or disapprobation.

We pursue the one, and avoid the other, by virtue of this inward and self-arising determination, and quite independent of any regard to the feelings or opinions of others. This latter (they say) may indeed appear as an auxiliary and a modifying influence, but it is not the primary ground of the determination : a man would find himself even from the beginning thus impelled and deterred, although there were no other being at hand to contemplate or criticise him.

This method of proceeding with regard to ethical sentiment appears to me erroneous and unphiloso-phical : *Erroneous*, because it altogether misconceives the actual genesis of the sentiment : *Unphilosophical*, because it diverts the attention from that which is common to ethical sentiment universally, in all times and places, to that in which it presents endless diver-sities and anomalies. That such diversities exist in respect to the various actions condemned, tolerated, and applauded, in different countries and ages, is a matter of incontestable notoriety : and he who pro-ceeds to render a general account of ethical senti-ment, taking for his basis of explanation the actions comprised under it, will find himself compelled to admit original and inherent diversities between the man of one age or country and the man of another. If this mode of explanation be applied only to those actions which are objects of moral approbation or of moral disapprobation, in all ages and countries, it will leave the largest portion of ethical sentiment not accounted for. If the same mode be extended to all —to the peculiar divergences of ethical sentiment as well as to the points of analogy, a thousand different characteristic instincts must be supposed discoverable some in one society and some in another. No philosopher, so far as I know, has yet contended for the supposition of all these multiplied and separate instincts : though it is a necessary and logical consequence of adopting the idea of the actions approved as the starting point of an explanatory theory— and thus rendering the *Form* of ethical sentiment secondary and subordinate to the *Matter*.

I believe that those who have represented our moral sentiments as an aggregate of original and unaccountable instincts, have clung to this theory mainly from a fear that the ethical motive would be degraded and enfeebled, if the sentiment out of which it arises were admitted to be derivative and generated by association. The authority of the moral sentiments (they imagined) would not be adequately sustained, unless the belief could be established that they were natural and ready-made instincts — impressed upon the mind directly by Nature herself, or by the Divine Author of Nature— original revelations, or direct commands and impulses, from the Divinity to man. Such seems to have been the idea of those who have insisted upon the doctrine of original and inexplicable instincts in morality. But the idea itself is altogether fallacious: nothing is gained in the way of authority by setting forth the ethical impulse as arising ready-made out of the hands of nature. They have this in common with many other impulses which carry with them no authority whatever, and which it is frequently necessary to disregard. All our appetites, and all our desires of relief from bodily uneasiness, are an inseparable part of our natural constitution: yet there is not one of these which we are justified in implicitly following: each of them must be so restrained and modified as to fall into harmony with our duty. If it were true, then, that our moral sentiments were implanted ready-made by nature, it would not be legitimate to infer that they ought implicitly to be obeyed: since nature implants in like manner numerous other impulses which it is indispensable often to resist. Nothing is acquired, in the way of authority, to the moral sentiments, by representing them as instinctive: on the contrary, much is lost: for by this supposition, all the separate divergences of the feeling are placed upon one common level, without the possibility of any standard for distinguishing fallacy from rectitude.

Are we to admit then that the moral sentiments are *factitious*? Quite the reverse. They are *derivative*, and generated by association from other simpler and more elementary principles of our nature : but the process of association by which they are formed is universal and uniform, so far as regards the *Form* of ethical sentiment: in regard to the *Matter*, it is to a high degree irregular and anomalous, but these anomalies are for the most part not *factitious*—they do not present the appearance of any separate premeditation or design. No instance has ever been presented to the actual observation of the historian, of families, previously destitute of all social training, coalescing with each other for the first time, and thus passing into a state of society. But it must have been during this period that all the languages now spoken on the globe must have taken their origin : and when we consider how complicated the mechanism is, both organical and mental, of the very simplest of these languages, we shall not be astonished that men who could overcome so vast a difficulty for the purposes of mutual communication, should be capable of conceiving in their minds the benefit of reciprocal help and the necessity of reciprocal abstinence from injury. If the semi-socialized man were capable of going through, and disposed to go through, those perplexing intellectual combinations on which the first construction of a language must have depended, *à fortiori* he must have been competent to conceive, and disposed to conceive, those simpler moral combinations which go to constitute ethical sentiment: more especially when we recollect that the latter process, after all, has been rudely and defectively performed, leaving out much, in regard to the *Matter*, which ought to have been taken in—and taking in, perhaps, still more which ought to have been left out.

The real difficulty in explaining ethical sentiment arises from these very irregularities in which the sentiment differs in one society and in another. But those who adopt the theory of instinct are so far from explaining such irregularities, that they leave them altogether unnoticed, and are not very willing to admit them in their full extent. It is quite impossible to account for them by any general theory. Each of them has had its special cause, in the early history of the people amongst whom it is found: but that cause has not been transmitted in history, and can very rarely be divined. Again, account must be taken of the connection of the early morality with religion, the Gods being looked upon as the great supplementary sanction for the enforcement of its observances. Acts pleasing or displeasing to the Gods come thus to be enrolled among the commands and prohibitions of morality: and this class of acts, depending entirely upon the temper and tastes which may happen to be ascribed to the Gods, differ materially when we pass from one people to another: they are not determined by human interests, and therefore there is no operative cause of uniformity.

With regard to the way in which ethical sentiment was first generated, on the original coalescence of rude men into a permanent social communion, we have no direct observation to consult, and must therefore content ourselves with assigning some unexceptionable theory. But with regard to the way in which ethical sentiment is sustained and transmitted, in a society once established, we have ample experience and opportunity for observing, before our eyes. We know perfectly that children are not born with any ethical sentiment : they acquire it in the course of early education, and we can trace the various stages of the process from its earliest rudiments to its complete maturity.

It will be impossible however to comprehend with any exactness either the real character or the true mode of generation, of ethical sentiment, unless we have previously familiarised ourselves with the principle of association in its great and fundamental modes of working. Two general truths are indisputably established and universally manifested in our various associative processes : First, that sensations and ideas which have been frequently experienced in conjunction, more especially if any one amongst them be vivid and interesting, have a tendency to run together into clusters or compounds, of which the

separate parts are not subjects of distinct consciousness : insomuch that unless we can retain a clear
recollection of some period of our lives when this
compound was unknown to us, we are apt to suppose
it a simple, original, and spontaneous, production
of the mind : Secondly, that sensations or ideas originally indifferent, when they have been long and
familiarly known as the causes, precursors, or concomitants of pleasure or pain, become at last pleasurable or painful in themselves : and that the idea
of what was at first only looked upon as the means
to pleasure or the precursor of pain, will very often
thus come to be more attractive or more terrible than
the original end. Many ideas, and many combinations of ideas, which originally affected us by a borrowed and secondary influence, acquire the power
of acting upon us directly and without any sensible
intermediation. They become magnetised (if one
may be allowed the metaphor) by frequent friction
and contact with the original and self-acting magnet :
and the new magnetic force thus created is often
greatly superior to the primary source from which
it is derived. Any act, or any state of existence,
which is profoundly impressed upon our minds as
the producing cause of an indefinite train of pleasures
or of pains, will become far more highly esteemed, or
far more intensely dreaded, than any definite lot of
the pleasures or pains to which it conducts.

These are the laws followed by the principle of association, in the generation of all that multiplicity of complex sentiments, opinions, and dispositions, which constitute the mental consciousness, and determine the actions, of every adult man. Amongst these complexities ethical sentiment is one—and one too, among the most complex of all—representing the result of many and various trains of emotion, and repeated processes of intellectual comparison superadded.

ESSAY II.

PHILOSOPHY OF MORALS.

PHILOSOPHY OF MORALS.

THERE are two enquiries which may be pursued with respect to systems of positive morality.

First, we may examine the various systems of positive morality with a view to ascertain what points they have in common, and what are the characteristic or distinctive points of each—wherein they resemble and wherein they differ : thus detecting those principles and distinctions which belong essentially to every system of positive morality, whether rude or refined, well or ill constructed.

Or, secondly, we may endeavour to determine the standard to which all systems of positive morality *ought* to conform, and according to which, in so far as they conform more or less to it, they are better or worse systems.

These are two distinct lines of enquiry, which may be pursued separately, and which ought not to be confounded ; though they often *are* confounded in such a manner that enquirers pass unconsciously from the one to the other.

Thus the question — *What constitutes morality?* may be so understood and treated as to belong sometimes to the first of these enquiries, sometimes to the second. You may either consider it as asking— What are the points common to all systems of actual positive morality? Or as asking—By what test are we to distinguish *right morality* from *wrong morality?*

But whether we pursue the one line of enquiry or the other, there is one distinction which is often forgotten and which it is of great importance to keep in mind.

Morality always implies two things : First, an individual agent supposed to act or to be capable of acting morally : Secondly, a public composed of spec-tators, or of parties interested in the tenor of his proceedings—by whose verdict, either really delivered or apprehended as possible, a rule of conduct is imposed upon the individual, or an artificial invita-tion held out to determine him.

There are thus two distinct points of view from which morality must be looked at—as it concerns the individual agent, and as it concerns the observing and judging public. Society requires from each individual person among its members a certain series of observances, and inflicts upon him, if he should omit them, censure, and refusal of good offices and sympathy, perhaps positive ill-treatment. Each individual occupies a double position : as a separate agent, he is himself under obligation to perform these duties to society : as a constituent member of society, he is engaged in enforcing the performance of them upon other individuals. Looking at morality from the point of view of society, it consists of an aggregate of duties commanded and enforced upon each individual : looking at it from the point of view of the individual, it consists of an aggregate of duties which he is bound to perform, whether performance be agreeable to him or not.

Positive morality, like positive law, always comprehends the three correlative notions, *command*, *duty*, and *sanction*. Society is the *superior* by whom commands are issued, duties imposed, and sanctions threatened or executed : the individual person is the *inferior*, by whom commands are received, duties performed or infringed, and sanctions endured or anticipated to be endured.

Positive morality, like positive law, must therefore be looked upon from two distinct points of view —according as it concerns the superior who issues orders, or the inferior who obeys them. It is impossible to resolve these two points of view into one, or to reason upon them as if they were the same. Society is the principal and the commanding party in regard both to positive law and to positive morality : the individual is the subordinate and subject party.

The ancient moralists seem to have more or less

committed the mistake of looking at morality exclusively from the point of view of the individual, and
not from the point of view of society. The *summum
bonum*, which they endeavoured to determine, and
which some of them determined in one manner, some
in another, had reference to individual agency.
They tried to instruct each individual agent as to
the object which he ought to aim at in life. They
estimated different objects as fit to be sought or
rejected in proportion to their value as affecting the
individual. They did not distinguish what was
imperative from what was optional : they addressed
themselves to the reason of each individual man, and
tried to prove to him that his own feelings and the
exigencies of his nature would be best satisfied by
a certain course of life such as they suggested.

This is undoubtedly one branch, and an important
branch, of every sufficient theory respecting morality. But it is not the real and genuine view in
which the theory of morality ought to be presented.
It suppresses the interests and feelings of society, in
order to give predominance to the interests and
feelings of the individual agent. Now it is of great
moment that the interests and feelings of each
individual agent should be brought to coincide as
much as possible with the exigencies of society, and
any line of argument which tends to this result is
useful. But still this is not the proper and genuine

representation of *any* system of positive morality. Every system of positive morality involves the idea of subjection on the part of the individual to the interests and feelings of society. It supposes that the majority of society concur in opinion as to certain duties incumbent upon each member individually, and thus constitute an authority competent to impose and enforce those duties. The foundation of morality lies in the collective opinions of the larger portion of society, not in the separate opinion of each individual agent with regard to his own good—just as the foundation of law lies in the command of the legislator who disposes of the force of society, not in the opinion of each individual as to the line of conduct which it may suit his views to pursue. Positive morality, as well as positive law, is conceived as superseding individual discretion. The idea of obligation or duty implies both a command and a sanction *from without,* against which the interior movements of individual inclination are not entitled to contend. This idea of an extraneous force, overriding the inclinations of the individual, constitutes what is called the supremacy of conscience, or the right of conscience to control the passions and inclinations of the individual, of which so much is said by Bishop Butler and Sir James Mackintosh. The authority of conscience, like the authority of law, is conceived as residing in a superior without—in the former case, as proceeding from the public—in the latter case, from the legislator. The idea of this authority, emanating from the public and extrinsic to the individual, is the paramount element of morality : the part of the individual is that of subordination or obedience to this authority.

If then, in any theory of morality, we omit the ideas of extrinsic authority, and obedience to such authority on the part of the individual, and explain it as only a well-directed choice and discretion on the part of the individual, we shall fall into a fundamental mistake. And this is the mistake committed by so many of the ancient moralists, when they laid the main stress on the ascertaining of the *summum bonum*, or of that which they would recommend to each individual as the primary object to aim at.

It may be contended perhaps that the supremacy which we ascribe to conscience cannot be considered as the idea of authority emanating from the public without, inasmuch as there are cases in which the conscience of the individual differs from the judgment of the public without, perhaps even conflicts with it pointedly.

But although individual conscience does thus occasionally conflict with the public judgment, it is not the less true that the authority which we ascribe to it is originally borrowed from the idea of approbation or disapprobation acting upon us from without. Conscience is the idea of moral approbation and disapprobation applied to our own actions or intentions: it comprehends the varieties of self-reproach, self-esteem, and self-admiration. Now this idea is based upon the actual fact that we find ourselves the objects of approbation and disapprobation on the part of others, and that we observe other individuals to be so also. The disapprobation of those around us is productive of painful consequences of the severest kind, and the idea of such a sentiment being entertained towards ourselves becomes painful in the highest degree: besides that we naturally come to partake, by means of sympathy, in the feelings which we see manifested by the persons among whom we are brought up. It is to be remarked that the feelings of approbation and disapprobation are in their nature essentially social, not personal feelings. They are not confined to our own bosoms: they essentially imply the concurrent sentiment of the public: and even if the actual public around us dissent from our views, we say that they ought to concur with us, and we carry in our minds the idea of a wiser and more enlightened public who would concur with us. In the large majority of cases, a man agrees in his particular acts of approbation and disapprobation with the public to which he belongs: if it were not so, there would be no public verdict on moral subjects. In this way, the idea of approbation and disapprobation becomes inseparably associated with that of a collective judgment pronounced by others as well as by ourselves. And if by virtue of any train of reasoning, or of any special authority, we come to dissent from the general public, and to attach the idea of approbation or disapprobation to certain acts with which the general public does not connect them, those ideas pass over with all their associated conjuncts and appendages, and present themselves as the voice of the public as it would be if the public were properly instructed. And in this manner the idea of the public voice *as it ought to be*, will often prevail over the idea of the public voice *as it is*.

The feeling of self-reproach, or of self-esteem, is, in other words, the feeling that we deserve or are likely to incur the reproach of others—that we deserve, or are likely to obtain, the esteem of others. Both the reproach and the esteem, though felt within the man's own mind, are imagined as proceeding from others.

There is also involved in the moral sentiment a feeling of implied reciprocity. The individual who feels it his duty to obey the command of the public without, feels himself entitled as one of the public to exact from every other individual the same observance as that to which he is himself submitting. Under the same circumstances as those in which he is placed, another man would be bound to perform the same duty now exacted from him. The order which the individual obeys is an order of equal and universal application to every one, given the like circumstances and position. If as an individual he is obliged to *obey*, as one of the public he is entitled to *enforce* upon other individuals.

This feeling of reciprocity between the *title to command* as one of the public, and the *obligation to obey* as an individual, is an essential element of the moral sentiment. You may look at it from either of the two points of view—either from that of the public or from that of the individual—and according as you look at it from the one or the other, it assumes a different aspect. But any theory which does not embrace *both* the points of view, is necessarily incomplete and erroneous.

In *positive law*, the mandate is issued by a determinate superior: the duty of the individual is to obey. The superior may perhaps be, but is not necessarily, a many-headed body, including the individual himself as a member. As an individual, he obeys laws which he has concurred in making and issuing.

In *positive morality*, the mandate is conceived as emanating from an indeterminate superior, a many-headed body called *the public*, of which the individual himself is necessarily and essentially a member. He obeys a mandate which as a member of this public he would concur in enforcing upon others. The idea of an external public concurring in judgment and dictation with himself, is essential: if the actual public around him should not partake in his convictions, he impeaches their verdict, he supposes that they would agree with him if they thoroughly meditated the circumstances of the case, and he imagines a better public concurrent with himself and constituting authority. This imaginary public he supposes to be as well acquainted with all the circumstances of his case and position as he is himself,—in fact much better acquainted than any real public can ever be—and it is to their verdict, thus perfectly instructed and enlightened, that he conforms his conduct.

If then we enquire what are the fundamental points common to all systems of positive morality, apart from the goodness or badness of any—we shall find them to consist in obedience on the part of an individual to commands from without, emanating from an indeterminate superior called the public, real or supposed, whereof the individual himself is a member. The feeling of obligation thus arising is strictly *moral obligation:* the command executed is a *moral command:* the sanction by which it is enforced is the *moral sanction,* consisting in the idea of approval or condemnation by a public without, concurring with the individual himself.

Kant is right in calling the maxim of moral agency *objective* and not *subjective*. That is, a man, who acts under a sense of moral obligation, believes that any other individual under the same circumstances would be under obligation to do the like. The obligation is equally and universally binding, whatever be the personal or peculiar inclinations of the individual.

Kant says that "Pure Reason is by itself alone (*i. e.* without the necessity of any conjunction of feeling or passion, *für sich allein*) practical, and gives to mankind an universal law which we call the Moral Law." (Prakt. Vern., p. 143.) This is only true in so far as reason is concerned in suggesting to a community of persons what actions they will forbid and what actions they will encourage. It is not reason which issues or gives the law, it is the community which gives the law, and which punishes neglect of the law by condemnation and disgrace.

Kant says farther, that in moral agency the *Bestimmungsgründe* of the will are *objective*, not *subjective*. This is true in a certain sense, but hardly in the sense in which he means it. When a man, under strong temptation to act immorally, resists and obeys the moral law, the matter of fact is, that the pain connected in his mind with the idea of disobeying the moral law is greater than the pain of resisting temp-

tation, and thus determines his behaviour. But this
sentiment is in every case a subjective sentiment—
that is, each individual experiences it in a degree
and manner peculiar to himself. There is indeed a
general similarity between the sentiment in one man
and in another man, which warrants us in calling
them by the same name, just as there is a similarity
between *hunger* and *fear* and *hope* in different individuals: but nevertheless each of these is in every
particular case a subjective affection.

Kant seems to think that the pains and pleasures
of the moral sentiments are not to be reckoned as
pains and pleasures : for this is what he means when
he says that morality carries with it no " *subjective
Bestimmungsgründe.*" He thinks that in the case of
the moral law, pure reason influences our will separately and by itself, without any admixture of feelings of pleasure or pain—in a manner inexplicable,
anomalous, and without parallel in our mental constitution.

But Kant seems to confound two things which
ought to be kept completely distinct. He confounds
the general painful idea associated in our minds with
an act of our own in violation of moral law—with
the anticipation of subsequent positive pains likely
to come upon us in consequence of such violation :
viz., the anticipation of punishment, loss of service,
loss of advancement, &c. It is very true that the

general painful idea, first mentioned, is derived by way of association from actual experience or observation of the positive pains last-mentioned as consequent on violations of duty. But still it is a feeling altogether distinct: it is an association which is formed in some minds and not formed in others: it is an association which when formed and when so firmly established as to govern the conduct, constitutes the truly *moral* man. A man in whose mind this association has not been formed, and who performs a moral obligation because he anticipates some positive loss or suffering in the event of his infringing it, cannot be said (as Kant observes) to act in the proper sense morally: his behaviour is *pflichtmässig*, but not *aus Pflicht*. But when we say that a man takes trouble or incurs risk or imposes upon himself privations because he feels called upon by his sense of duty—what we really mean is, that the painful feeling, associated in his mind with the idea of violating his duty, is of greater force with him than the idea of the pain which he is to encounter in performing it. The ideas of self-reproach—of subsequent mental remorse—of the loss of his title to the esteem and confidence of others—of not being able to hold up his head in the company of others, because he has done what renders him unworthy of their respect—all these are highly painful. On the other hand, the ideas of self-esteem—of subsequent mental approbation—of having acquired increased title to the esteem and confidence of others, and holding up his head higher than ever in their presence, because he has performed his duty under the most trying circumstances and the strongest temptation to evade it—all these are ideas highly gratifying, and at the very least consolatory under suffering. It is not meant to say that the performance of duty under these supposed circumstances will be anything but painful : the man is placed in a position in which nothing is open to him except the choice between two modes of conduct both of which are painful. He does not do right because it is agreeable to him to do so : but because the idea of doing wrong is more painful to him than the idea of the sufferings consequent upon his doing right.

Moral action is not to be at all considered as an exception to the general rules of human conduct. The man who acts morally acts just as much under the influence of ideas of pleasure and pain, as the man who acts immorally : only his pleasures and pains are different. The pleasures and pains of conscience are among the most remarkable and important of all human emotions. Any philosophical system which takes no account of them or denies their existence, must of necessity be very defective. We know that they often amount to torture or extasy—" Si recludantur tyrannorum mentes, posse

aspici laniatus et ictus."—" Mens sibi conscia facti,
Præmetuens, adhibet stimulos, torretque flagellis."—
" Virtus, si videri posset, mirabiles amores sui ipsius
concitaret." Many other similar metaphors might
be cited, which illustrate the extent of gratification
as well as of suffering arising out of the conscience.
When a man acts morally, the idea of these pleasures
and pains constitutes the *Bestimmungsgrund* of his
behaviour—what Kant calls *Achtung für das Gesetz*
—a regard for *den Werth seiner Person* as contradistinguished from *den Werth seines Zustandes*. His
own sense of self-esteem is inseparably connected
with his observance of the moral law. But a man's
sense of self-esteem is only another word to express
the feeling which he has of that esteem which he
ought to receive from others—which the public
would award to him, if they were perfectly right-
minded and thoroughly acquainted with all the
circumstances of the case.

Kant, in speaking of morality, considers it as a
single and anomalous case of what he calls the *Autonomy* of the will, in contradistinction to the *Heteronomy* which in every other case of action of the
will is observable. In the sense in which he intends
this remark, I think it is not correct. He means by
Autonomy, that there are in this case no conside-
rations of pleasure or pain influencing the will—in
this case *alone*. I do not agree in this opinion. It

appears to me that the will is in this case as in all others, determined by the pleasures or pains associated with our ideas of obeying or disobeying the moral law; called usually the sense of duty or Conscience.

But there is undoubtedly a sense in which the observation of Kant is partly true. Under the influence of a sense of duty, my will is determined to aim at the accomplishment of a given object. I employ my most strenuous efforts—I do every thing which can possibly be expected of me—for the purpose of accomplishing it: but I fail. Notwithstanding the failure, the exigencies of the moral sentiment are satisfied. Provided the failure is not owing to any want of prudence, or skill, or persevering energy, an enlightened conscience finds nothing to disapprove. Though the sense of duty at the outset commands and determines me to do my best, it is after all satisfied without the realization of the end originally sought. Sincere, hearty, and energetic obedience to the moral law is all which is required: what Kant calls *ein reiner Wille*, explained in the way that he defines it, though the expression is a very misleading one. My will, or my desire, is unsatisfied, because the object is not attained: but the sense of duty in which my desire originated, is nevertheless satisfied, if every thing within the limits of possibility has been done to attain it. The pleasures and pains of self-esteem are associated, not with the attainment of the object, but with the doing, or omitting to do, every thing which skill and zeal can suggest for such a purpose.

Now it is in this respect that the term *Autonomy* of the Will, as contradistinguished from *Heteronomy*, has a certain application. Our pleasures and pains generally are derived from the attainment of various objects foreign to ourselves: we desire these objects and try to attain them: our gratification depends upon success. The pleasures and pains of the moral sense, on the other hand, are not derived from the positive attainment of any object foreign to ourselves: they are derived from reflection on our own conduct in the pursuit of it. The satisfaction of the moral sentiment is independent of the actual result: it is not contingent upon success or failure: no external impediments can disappoint it. The will is determined, not by the idea of a certain object necessary to be obtained, but by the idea of a certain line of conduct necessary to be pursued by ourselves: it is therefore in a certain sense *autonomous*, not *heteronomous*.

In another sense, also, the expression *autonomous* may be used. The moral law is a command which a man in conjunction with the public imposes upon himself. He acts in obedience to his own sentiment in harmony with what either actually is, or what he thinks ought to be, the sentiment of the public. If he obeys the command of the public simply, his own sentiment not concurring with it, this is not properly moral acting—it is *pflichtmässig*, but not *aus Pflicht*: it is heteronomy and not autonomy. Properly speaking moral acting is both the one and the other: the man himself, concurring with a public, real or ideal.

ESSAY III.

ANCIENT SYSTEMS OF MORAL PHILOSOPHY.

ANCIENT SYSTEMS OF MORAL PHILOSOPHY.

THE ancient systems of Ethics took for their start-ing point mainly, and primarily, the happiness or *summum bonum* of the individual. It was assumed, and admitted by each of the dissenting schools of philosophy, that every individual would pursue his own happiness or his own *summum bonum :* but as different individuals entertained different views respecting the summum bonum, the problem for philosophers was, to determine wherein the real summum bonum consisted—what was that End of Ends which it was best for every individual separately taken to aim at, and which if he attained, he was to be pronounced perfectly happy ?

It is undoubtedly true that the ancients did not adopt this point of view exclusively. They con-sidered the sentiments and actions of each individual to a certain extent as affecting others as well as himself; as imparting to others enjoyment or misery, and creating in them gratitude or resentment. But still in the main, the primary point of view, the

ethical *Standpunkt* of the ancients, was the position
and condition of the agent himself. To advise him
as to the means requisite for becoming happy, was
the grand ethical problem.

Nothing can more clearly evince the preponderance
of this point of view than the tenacity with which
even the Stoics adhered to it, though it involved
them in the greatest perplexities and enabled their
opponents to taunt them with glaring contradictions.
It was absolutely indispensable, in their opinion, to
prove that virtue and nothing else produced a happy
life to the individual: if this could not be shewn,
they admitted that their whole system was worth-
less. Cato is made to say (in Cicero de Finib. iii. 3)
—"Nam si hoc non obtineatur, id solum. bonum
esse, quod honestum sit; nullo modo probari possit,
beatam vitam virtute effici : quod si ita sit, *cur
opera philosophiæ sit danda, nescio :* si enim sapiens
aliquis miser esse possit, næ ego istam gloriosam
memorabilemque virtutem non magni æstimandam
putem."

But though the ancient moralists thus selected the
condition of the individual agent as the ἀρχὴ of their
various ethical systems, they explained it in such a
way as to alter very materially those conclusions
which might naturally be expected to flow from such
a principle. The end which each individual both
did pursue and ought to pursue was admitted to be

happiness: but different persons took different views as to the constituent elements of happiness. Now the ancient philosophers did not admit that each man was the proper judge and measure of happiness in his own individual case. They maintained that there was a right and a wrong choice upon this point— that one man might and did choose better than another,—and that the wise and virtuous man was the only legitimate referee. That man alone was understood to be happy, whom the wise man pronounced to be happy, and whose condition he would have been willing to adopt as his own : that man alone was understood to be unhappy, whom the wise man declared to be unhappy, and whose character and position he was disposed to repudiate. The Summum Bonum, or grand end which every man ought to aim at, was happiness according to the scheme laid down by the wise man : the Summum Malum, or that which it was proper for every man to avoid, was Unhappiness in the sense in which the wise man defined it.

According to the schemes of the ancient moralists, it seems that a man might be happy or unhappy, though he neither felt nor believed himself to be so. At least the man's own sentiments and belief were not regarded as the proper measure and evidence of happiness. He might himself be perfectly well satisfied and even strongly attached to his condition :

yet the wise man might not recognise him as happy.
Or he might be in a state from which he was very
anxious to escape, and yet the wise man might
refuse to pronounce him unhappy. Seneca indeed
(Epist. IX.) seems to say the contrary of this, and
to cite both Epicurus and the Stoics as authorities—
"Non est beatus, esse se qui non putat"—and
then he eludes the difficulty by contending—"Nisi
sapienti sua non placent : omnis stultitia laborat fas-
tidio sui."

In appreciating the moral systems of the ancients,
however, it is of great moment to keep in view the
way in which they understood and defined *Happiness*.
The ethical ἀρχὴ from which they started was, the
injunction upon every individual to pursue his own
happiness. But this, if allowed to be interpreted by
the individual himself, would have led to endless
errors and deviations, according to every man's
different taste. Accordingly they laid down the
scheme of one particular state of mind and circumstances, as constituting the maximum of individual
happiness, or the only thing which they were willing
to call happiness. Each of the philosophical sects
did this, though all of them did not lay down the
same scheme. To pursue happiness, was to follow
the scheme of happiness prescribed by the wise man :
whoever did not follow this, whatever his own tastes
or inclinations might be, was not allowed to be

obeying the natural dictate of pursuing his own happiness.

It is easy to see that when the definition of happiness was so restricted as to embrace only that which the wise man would call happiness, the main observances of morality would be quite sure to be comprehended in it. The wise and virtuous man would not esteem any other man happy who was not wise and virtuous. He might perhaps not account another man happy with wisdom and virtue alone, though accompanied by great external disadvantages : but the presence of these lofty mental qualities he would deem absolutely indispensable.

The ancient moralists considered the happiness of the individual agent as the sole and exclusive end : but they also considered that virtuous conduct was the sole and exclusive means to that end. In this manner the interests and happiness of persons other than the individual came to be inseparably intermingled in their theories with the interests and happiness of the individual himself, although the latter alone formed the original point of departure.

In studying their moral treatises, this confusion will often be found both very prevalent and very perplexing. When they speak of *good*, it is sometimes *good* with reference to the interests and happiness of the individual agent—sometimes *good*, with reference to the interests and happiness of society.

The ancient philosophers pass from the one to the other without any preliminary warning, and seemingly without consciousness of any transition whatsoever. If a man has achieved some great and glorious deed, both deserving and obtaining the admiration of the society to which he belongs, they consider him as having attained a considerable *good* —as having *placed* himself in a situation to be macarised by the wise and virtuous—without taking account of the personal sacrifices which he may have undergone in the performance, and which may have been so intolerably painful as to make the result a matter of no happiness at all, judging by his individual sentiments. Whatever the sentiments of the individual might be, the moralist ventured to speak for him, according to a general rule determined beforehand, and to vest the decision in the wise and virtuous man. An indisputable *good* has been done, looking at the case from the point of view of the society : the wise and virtuous man takes upon himself to pronounce, without farther enquiry, that the agent has acquired a portion of *good*, and that he deserves to be considered happy.

I do not mean to say that this confusion of ideas is universally obvious throughout the works of the ancient moralists. At times they seem to get clear of it, especially Aristotle : there are occasions on which they admit that what is good for the individual agent may not always be good for others besides him, and *vice versâ*. But still their ordinary mode of reasoning is to confound the two, and to employ the words *good* and *happiness* as if they neither had nor could have more than one standard of reference.

Both Plato and the Stoics must be considered to have neglected the sentiments of the individual agent, when they laid it down in so unqualified a manner that the man who acted virtuously could never be miserable, and that the man who acted viciously could not be happy. At least they presupposed a very peculiar and a very efficacious training, carried so far as almost to efface from the mind the ordinary measure of self-regarding sentiment. Aristotle requires a certain measure of training and acquired habits, as a necessary preliminary to the appreciation of ethical motives : but not to the same extent which would be requisite to fulfil the theories of Plato and the Stoics : who, although professing to adopt for their ἀρχή or starting point the happiness of the individual agent himself, ended in taking no account at all of his feelings, except in so far as they coincided with those of the virtuous and right-minded spectator.

It is altogether impossible to reason correctly upon ethical subjects, unless you admit two distinct and independent ἀρχαὶ of reasoning. 1. The happiness of persons other than the agent himself. 2. The happiness of the agent individually.

These two *ends of action*, or *beginnings of ethical reasoning*, are sometimes found in conflict, but more frequently in coincidence : but they are by no means co-ordinate, or of equal weight and dignity in the eyes of the moralist. When both cannot be attained, the happiness of the individual must be postponed, as a general rule, to that of the community to which he belongs.

These are the two sole ἀρχαὶ of ethical science. Every action which is wrong or blameworthy, is so because it tends to impair either the happiness of the individual himself or that of others, perhaps of both at once. Every action which is right or praiseworthy, is so because it tends to promote one or both of these ends : an action indeed may have such tendency, without being necessarily praiseworthy : but no action can be praiseworthy, unless it conform to the condition here described.

Strictly speaking, it is doubtful whether any action whatever is a proper subject either of praise or blame. The agent who performs it is the proper subject of praise or blame, according to his intention and knowledge : the action itself is useful or hurtful, but it cannot be said either to be right or wrong : it is an action such as a virtuous man would do, or such as only a vicious man would do, but it is not in itself either virtuous or vicious.

The moralist, or ethical philosopher, who takes

upon him to explain and criticise the different tempers, dispositions, and capacities which discriminate one individual from another, must be assumed to address himself to the whole society, and not to any special individual exclusively. His business is to consider the conduct and dispositions of each separate individual, in so far as that conduct and those dispositions bear upon the happiness both of the individual himself and of others. He is therefore called upon to consider every separate man, on the one hand, as an agent in himself, under the influence of certain dispositions which provoke to action or deter from action—on the other hand, as a person affected by his own actions, either singly or in conjunction with other members of the community. Each person separately and indiscriminately comes before the ethical philosopher in these two different points of view. This therefore suggests naturally the double classification of actions above alluded to—

1. Actions which tend to impair, or to promote, the happiness of the public—meaning by the *public* any fraction, large or small, of the society, not even excluding the agent himself as one of the number.

2. Actions which tend to impair, or to promote, the happiness of the agent himself separately : I mean permanently and in the long run, as distinguished from the gratification of his immediate impulse.

These are the two classifications of actions and of dispositions which form the canon of criticism in ethical philosophy.

The two systems of arrangement may either coincide or clash, in any particular case. In the long run, and with reference to the greater number of actions and dispositions, they do coincide: for it is obvious that what tends to promote the happiness of the public must tend to promote the happiness of the greater number of individuals among the public, separately and indiscriminately taken. One of these two propositions is included in the other.

But though generally coincident, the two systems of arrangement are always liable to clash in particular cases and with regard to any particular individual. An action which tends to promote the happiness of the agent may not impair that of others : an action which greatly impairs the happiness of the agent may be necessary to prevent that of the society from being impaired in a still greater degree.

When the two systems of classification clash, it is necessary for the ethical philosopher to determine which of the two he will prefer : whether he will rather encourage that which tends to the happiness of the agent or that which tends to the happiness of the society—whether he will discourage that which impairs the former or that which impairs the latter.

When the case is thus nakedly stated, there cannot

be the smallest hesitation which of the two ends is to
be preferred. It is possible indeed by means of a
cloud of unmeaning words to perplex the question
and to disguise the real nature of the alternative :
but when properly understood, the two things to be
compared are the same which have just been stated,
and the choice is therefore simple and easy. When
the alternative lies between suffering experienced by
the community on the one side—and either suffering
experienced, or the foregoing of happiness, by any
particular agent on the other—the latter must be
submitted to in order to escape the former.

Hence is derived the authority of what is called
the moral sense—the force of moral obligation. The
ethical philosopher addresses himself to each individual in the name of the community, and he
therefore speaks to each in a tone of command and
supremacy. When the happiness of the society
requires that a certain act shall be done or left
undone, he does not leave with the individual agent
the option of performance or omission. The interests of the community are paramount, and the ethical
philosopher, as representing that community, exacts
obedience on the part of the agent, whether such
obedience be easy or painful. This is the source of
the *moral imperative :* it is a voice representing the
entire community, and addressed to an agent who is
one of its members. The right of the community to

exact obedience from each of its own individual members, in cases where its serious interests are concerned, is a matter which the ethical philosopher assumes from the beginning : he never attempts to demonstrate it. Without this right in fact society could not subsist : *positive law* is one of the forms in which it is exercised, *positive morality* is another.

If we take the greater number of individual agents in the greater number of cases—saving always particular exceptions both of individuals and of cases— it may be said generally that the agent himself feels in his own bosom the obligation to render obedience to a command so issued in the name and for the interests of the community. He is himself one of that community, and he has been accustomed in other cases to concur in imposing the like obligation upon others. He cannot fail to apply to himself more or less the same remarks which he would have made upon another agent placed in similar circumstances. But whether he does so or not, the obligation does not the less exist, in the view of the ethical philosopher : it does not depend upon feeling or absence of feeling on the part of the agent.

The *moral imperative*, and the *legal imperative*, have their origin in the same relations and in the same necessity. In each case control is exercised by or on behalf of the entire community over one of its members : in each case the relation of supremacy of the whole over any part is implied : in each case the necessity of ensuring protection and happiness to the community, even at the cost (if such be unavoidable) of the happiness of any individual, is assumed as self-evident.

In fact, prior to the establishment of written laws and fixed judges, the whole of what is now positive law was in the condition of that which is now positive morality. The commencement of writing was not farther removed from the days of Aristotle and Plato, than that of printing is from us.

ESSAY IV.

IDEA OF ETHICAL PHILOSOPHY.

IDEA OF ETHICAL PHILOSOPHY.

I.

ETHICS, in the most extended sense, is the science of human dispositions, emotions, desires, and actions, in so far as they affect, or are regarded by society as affecting, either the happiness of the individual himself, or the happiness and sentiments of others. All these common characteristics of our nature are manifested in a different degree and manner and arise out of different circumstances, in one man and in another. Besides these individual differences, there are also local and national differences which distinguish one society from another: the members of the same society are found to resemble each other in the turn of their feelings, and to differ in the same respect from the members of other societies: in so much that certain general propositions may be affirmed or denied of each.

To explain the nature and origin of these different feelings—to trace them both to their causes and their consequences—to shew by what circumstances they are encouraged, repressed, or modified—to explain that which all ethical systems have in common, as well as the distinguishing features of each as compared with another, and to assign as far as may be the producing causes of such diversity—to classify and denominate conveniently all these complicated emotional phenomena—this is the scope and business of the ethical philosopher. It is plain that this is a subject of vast extent, co-extensive with the whole field of human action and even of human feeling. For the ethical criticisms actually current in a community are liable to embrace every part of a man's conduct and dispositions, not merely where other persons are concerned, but even where he himself alone is directly concerned. And none of these ethical criticisms can properly be omitted in a complete system of ethical philosophy.

But there is also another part of the province of the ethical philosopher which, while intimately connected with the preceding, is yet perfectly distinguishable from it. He is not simply an observer and expositor : he is also a *critic*. He is to explain how far each disposition and emotion tends to the happiness or misery both of the person experiencing it and of others, and how far therefore each deserves to be fostered or counteracted. He is to suggest means for stifling, as far as may be, the noxious liabilities of our nature, and for improving all its beneficent tendencies. These tendencies do indeed exist, independently of his choice or observation : but they admit of being greatly modified, either for the better, or for the worse, by circumstances within our control. The *critical function* of the ethical philosopher consists in bringing out clearly this *better*, and *worse*, and in accustoming others, as far as may be, to recognise and aim at it.

The *expository* function, and the *critical* function, are decidedly distinct, but they are nevertheless intimately connected. The critical both assists and presupposes the expository. First, it assists, by teaching what phenomena are to be observed. The sum total of effects produced by any passion or disposition, is infinitely large, and the man who would observe to any purpose must know how to separate the important effects from the unimportant. Now the importance or non-importance of the effects is measured by their influence upon the happiness or misery of the agent himself or of others. Unless therefore the ethical philosopher, considered as an observer, be accustomed to conduct his observations with reference to this canon, he will not be able to distinguish what is important or unimportant for the purposes even of exposition.

Next, the critical function presupposes the expository. You cannot criticise any disposition or emotion, unless you know previously what it is and what are its effects. You cannot point out the means of encouraging or repressing it, unless you know the circumstances under which it is usually generated.

Both these functions — the expository and the critical—are essential to ethical philosophy. Both have always been attempted, in point of fact, more or less perfectly, even in the rudest essays of ethical philosophy, and in the most ancient times. It is scarcely possible for any adult person, be he philosopher or not, to speak of human dispositions without feeling some sentiment and intimating some judgment of his own respecting them. But though neither of the two functions is altogether omitted, they often become inconveniently confounded : a man explains the historical origin of certain dispositions and sentiments, and thinks that by so doing he has justified them critically : or he expatiates upon the value of certain dispositions and sentiments as admirable portions of our nature, and thinks that by so doing he is dispensed from the necessity of studying or expounding their origin. In this manner, although a writer unites the two functions of criticism and exposition, yet he is never conscious to himself where the one begins or where the other ends ; nor does he even seem aware that the very attempt to criticise necessarily implies an assumed standard of judgment selected by himself. Thus, for example, the most serious confusion arises between criticism and exposition in respect to the use of the term *nature* and *natural*. To say of any sentiment or disposition, that it is *natural*, is thought to be the same as saying that it is justifiable and becoming : though the most mischievous sentiments in the human mind are no less *natural* than the most beneficent.

The question has often been asked, *Upon what is moral obligation founded?* To this question different answers have been returned. But I think the question is somewhat ambiguous, in the terms in which it is put. The root from which the sentiment of obligation springs, in the mind of each individual person, is, the absolute necessity of avoiding the displeasure of those around him and of conciliating a certain measure of their esteem and kindness. A man feels himself under obligation to do such actions and to manifest such dispositions, as are necessary to accomplish this end. In time the feeling with which he originally regarded the end, comes to be transferred to the means : he feels obliged to perform the action, without any distinct or separate consciousness of the ulterior purpose which the action was first intended to serve. Such is the original source of the feeling of obligation, as it exists in the bosom of each individual : it is a feeling not arising out of the inherent and intrinsic attributes of the action, but out of the effect which the performance of the action is calculated to produce upon the sentiments of others.

But if the same question be put to the ethical philosopher—*Upon what is ethical obligation founded?* —the answer which he will return will be different. To the individual agent, the pronounced sentiment of the society to which he belongs, when intense and unanimous, is final and without appeal: he cannot escape from the necessity of obeying it, whatever be the character of its injunctions. But the ethical philosopher will feel both inclined and authorized to push his enquiries farther. He will examine upon what foundation those commands and prohibitions of the society which constitute irresistible authority for the individual agent, are founded. In his view, there is no legitimate foundation for these commands and prohibitions, except their tendency to promote the safety, happiness, and enjoyment of the society. This is the answer he will make to the question: Upon what is founded ethical obligation? He will consider ethical obligation as it would be if mankind were perfectly wise and right-minded: he will find that a society composed of men in such a stage of improvement, would enforce no prohibitions or commands, except such as tended to promote their safety, their happiness, and their enjoyment; that they would hate and condemn only such agents as were likely to counteract these ends: and that they would esteem and favour different agents in proportion as they tended to assist these same ultimate purposes.

The ethical philosopher, conceiving the idea of a society wiser and better than any actually existing, is able to detect one single and assignable foundation for all the various ordinances of ethical sanction— viz. : the safety and happiness of the society. Taking men as they are now, no such single foundation can be made to fit : we must acquiesce in the existing sentiment of the community, as the ultimate basis of ethical obligation : we can only say that the greater part of the ethical sanctions have a converging tendency towards the happiness of society as their end, not that all of them distinctly point to it and acknowledge it as paramount.

Nor is it to be expected, indeed, that in the existing condition of humanity, all the separate forces of sanction should actually be aimed with exclusive reference to this end, any more than that all the separate forces of legislative sanction as it now exists are directed towards it : although in the eye of the philosopher, happiness is the only legitimate end towards which the sanctions legislative as well as ethical *ought* to be directed.   When a philosopher lays it down, that the only proper end for which the legislative sanction ought to be employed is the happiness of the society—it is no sufficient reply to this position to point out, that legislation as it now stands is not in fact directed exclusively towards this end.   The philosopher will admit the truth of this answer as a matter of fact, but he will deny its force as a refutation. If it be not so (he will say) it ought to be so, and it will be so when men become improved. The like reply may be made with respect to ethical sanction, which, as men are now constituted, is certainly not directed exclusively towards the promotion of the social happiness. That this is true now, and always has been true, as a matter of fact is no ground of opposition to the philosopher who contends that it *ought* to be so.

Besides, it is admitted on all hands that the observance of ethical obligations is absolutely indispensable to ensure the safety and happiness of society ; without such observance these ends could not possibly be attained. It may be said that these are not the *only* ends which ethical observances answer—it may further be said that they are ends attained not by any deliberate foregoing consciousness, but by hap-hazard. But still it is not the less true that the safety and happiness of society are the actual result of the establishment of ethical relations among its members, and that every adult person has a conviction that they are so.

Moreover, this grand end is common to all the separate exhibitions of ethical sentiment, in all times and places. The positive morality of one age agrees in this respect with the positive morality of another. But in respect to other accessory ends, not connected with the safety and happiness of society, the morality of one age differs very widely from that of another. There are endless divergences in matters of peculiar fancy and sentiment.

As positive morality has existed up to the present time, there are such accessory ends in every society, sometimes occupying as much attention as the main end. If we collect the list of all actions which are either approved or disapproved, esteemed or abhorred, it will not be found that *all* in the former list are actions which tend to the safety or happiness of the society—still less will it be found that all the latter list are actions which tend to the peril or misery or discomfort of the society. Such predicates will be true with regard to a certain number of the actions comprised in each list — but certainly not with regard to all.

That men have a tendency to love and esteem those beings who are causes of happiness to them, and to hate and dread those who occasion them suffering, is unquestionable. This is a tendency common to all mankind and observable in every different society. In so far as men feel and judge under the influence of this tendency, the positive morality of all societies is cast nearly upon the same mould, and assumes similar features.

But there are two points to be considered in addition to this general statement.

First, men do not always rightly apprehend the causes of their happiness or misery. They fancy certain things and persons to be causes of these results, which in reality are not so—and *vice versâ*.

Secondly, it is not merely the causes of happiness which have a tendency to become objects of our love and esteem, but all those accessories which have become associated in our minds as concomitant with happiness. It is not merely the causes of misery which have a tendency to become objects of our hatred and fear, but all those accessories which have become associated as concomitant with misery.

These two last-mentioned circumstances greatly modify the course and direction of ethical sentiment, and occasion wide divergences between different societies. One society has been led by some accidental and forgotten reason, to fix upon one accessory as the object of esteem or abhorrence : another society upon another. The mistakes made by different societies, in overlooking causes real and assigning causes supposed, are not always the same. Hence the positive morality of one age or one society comes to vary in many material respects from that of another. And when once any special ethical antipathy has become rooted in a society, it transmits itself from generation to generation, with scarcely any chance of being ever eradicated.

Although therefore the ethical sentiment is one

formed by association, we are not to expect, even according to the laws of association, that it should be framed accurately and exclusively upon the basis of utility, except in a society which has reached the highest pitch of mental improvement. The erroneous ethical sentiment is just as much formed by a process of association as the sound ethical sentiment: only that the former results from associations accidental, capricious, and involving mistakes of fact—the latter results from associations general, common to all mankind, capable of being arranged in an harmonious system, and sure to increase in force and authority as society becomes more instructed.

To collect and compare together the positive morality of different societies, has a tendency to enlarge and purify the character of ethical sentiment, and to disengage those great principles which are common to all ages and nations from the capricious adjuncts which are peculiar to this or that portion of the globe. The grand features of morality acquire increased and peculiar dignity in our minds, in consequence of our finding them everywhere reproduced and everywhere more or less venerated : we become gradually familiarised with the idea of a standard of morality, different from that actually prevalent anywhere, by which the positive morality of each particular nation is to be tried. We are thus brought many stages nearer, to say the least of it, to the principle of utility.

If we take the law of nature, or ethical sentiment as it pervades all mankind, it may be stated with very little exception, that this universal morality is founded upon the same universal cause—the absolute necessity of its rules for the protection of the safety and happiness of society. But if we take ethical sentiment as it exists in any given society, we cannot assign any determinate foundation upon which it rests. The sentiment exists, apparently without any foundation; that is, we cannot trace all its different manifestations to any one common principle.

Ethical sentiment may be traced partly to the self-regarding tendencies of our nature—partly to the antipathetic tendencies. 1. To the self-regarding tendencies, in so far as the favour and esteem of others, to a certain extent, is absolutely essential to our preservation and comfort. 2. To the sympathetic tendencies, in so far as we thereby conceive and partake the feelings of others—in so far as we thereby conceive and become attached to a common interest between ourselves and them—and in so far as we love the causes of safety and happiness to others as well as to ourselves. 3. To the antipathetic tendencies, in so far as we hate the causes of pain to ourselves—and by sympathetic antipathy (if one may say so), the cause of pain to others.

What is called the *moral faculty* (and indeed the word *faculty* generally) is a very ambiguous expression ; it is generally understood to indicate something *ready made*, not gradually formed—something implanted by nature, not gradually acquired. If it be meant, by saying that man has a *moral faculty*, simply to affirm that he is so organized, and placed in such circumstances, as that he will assuredly in the course of a certain time form ethical associations, I admit this perfectly : I also admit that these ethical associations form a class by themselves, distinguishable from every other modification of our consciousness, so that it is proper and necessary to bestow upon them a separate denomination. But it is not the less true that ethical sentiment is a highly complex association, composed of many different ideas and many different feelings united together intimately and indissolubly, undergoing successive modifications according as our experience is enlarged and according as we apply it to new cases. It involves both a group of feelings and a process of reason ; for the constant necessity of dealing with new cases renders some exercise of reason inevitable. In order to conduct himself with propriety in any new case, a man is forced to put together in his mind the various analogies which his former experience has presented to him, and to apply the result to the case before him. This cannot be done without an intellectual process more or less perfectly performed—performed too by the aid of general terms, which presuppose a classification of actions and dispositions, reposing upon some fixed principle. There is both a process of feeling and a process of reason superadded—the latter capable of being stated in general terms.

II.

We have records of certain observed states of society, existing at various times and in various places, in which there have been no written law and no established or permanent judges. In such cases a large portion of what is now the province of legis-lation would be left as a portion of the wide field of positive morality. If under such circumstances a man abstained from theft, this would arise not from the fear of legal punishment, but either from repug-nance in his own mind, or from fear of resentment on the part of the sufferer, or from a dread of the unfavourable sentiments of the society around him. Theft would then be an immoral act; and the dis-position to thieve, an immoral disposition. When a law is made prohibiting theft, or when judges are named who are empowered to punish every act of theft, the act of theft becomes illegal, but without ceasing to be immoral; the disposition to thieve continues to be immoral as it was before—it cannot be calledillegal, for neither legislators nor judges can meddle with dispositions except in so far as they are manifested and reduced into action.

In the outset of legislation, it is probable that few or no acts would be made illegal or punished, except such acts as were previously deemed immoral by the feelings of the society. But in process of time and as society proceeds, it is found convenient to establish a fixed rule in cases where doubt and uncertainty produce confusion, although the rule selected is perhaps not in itself better than many other rules equally applicable. As the authority of legislators and judges became established, many acts and many omissions were in this manner declared to be illegal and punished, although previously they were in no way immoral. Being however once declared illegal by competent authority, they became immoral more or less. This characteristic coincides with that which Aristotle applies to νομικὸν δίκαιον (conventional justice) as opposed to φυσικὸν δίκαιον (natural justice). ὃ ἐξ ἀρχῆς μὲν οὐθὲν διαφέρει, οὕτως ἢ ἄλλως, ὅταν δὲ θῶνται, διαφέρει (Ethic. Nic. v. 7).

One portion of the domain occupied by legislation is thus formed of matter which previously belonged to the field of Ethics : another portion is formed of matter which did not previously belong to the field of Ethics, but which ˉcomes afterwards to belong to it in consequence of having been determined by legislative precept.

The *positive* morality of any given age or nation consists of the opinions and feelings then current respecting what is right or wrong—blameable, indifferent or praiseworthy—respectable or contemptible or ridiculous—becoming or unbecoming—suitable or unsuitable to any given character or position —and to a certain extent also, of that which is graceful and elegant, or unpleasing and repulsive. Each individual has sentiments of this sort, according to which he judges both his own conduct and disposition and that of others. The sentiments with which we regard what we think right, praiseworthy, respectable, becoming, suitable, &c., is one of satisfaction as applied to ourselves, of favour as applied to others: that with which we regard the contrary, is a sentiment of discomfort, sometimes even of the most acute pain, as applied to ourselves—of aversion or perhaps intense hatred as applied to others. The desire to acquire this favour, and the fear of incurring this repulsion, are among the most powerful motives to action known to human nature. Both the actual feeling as applied to a case or agent really before us, and the idea of that feeling as applied to a case yet unrealized and contingent either upon our own determination or upon that of others, is called by the name *moral sentiment*. And the idea of the pleasurable or painful feeling, constitutes the desire, or aversion, which serves as a motive to and from action.

The ethical feeling properly so called is essentially a *social* sentiment, capable of being felt by every one man in the community towards every other man, and not implying any special community or fraternity between the two. The affection which may prevail between two brothers or two friends is not, in the proper sense of the word, an ethical sentiment, any more than the special antipathy which may happen to subsist between two personal enemies. The judgment or sentiment with which the spectators around, who are not personally concerned, regard this affection or antipathy — and the sort of self-judgment with which the parties concerned regard themselves in consequence of their knowledge of what other people are feeling in respect to them— this is properly the *ethical* or moral *sentiment*. The ethical or moral sentiment is one in which every individual around, or even the whole world, might be conceived as capable of sharing. The very basis and primary element of ethical sentiment is expected and assured reciprocity of conduct and disposition. I know that I desire to receive certain benefits, and to be the object of certain affections and dispositions, on the part of others: I know that I hate to experience harm or to be the object of certain other dispositions and affections on their part. I believe that others desire the same conduct and sentiments, and wish to avert the same conduct and sentiments, from me towards them. I also believe that every individual amongst the persons around me has the same desires and the same aversions with respect to other persons, me included. That I should manifest towards others that conduct and disposition which they wish to re-ceive from me—and that I should receive from them that conduct and those dispositions which I desire from them—the two phenomena being indissolubly linked together under the sanction of a superintend-ing and extraneous force—this it is which constitutes *ethical sentiment*.

It is a feeling of certain *obligations* under which I stand, and of certain *rights* which I enjoy, each con-ditionally upon the other and mutually implying the other ,and both guaranteed by a common enforcing sanction.

Ethical sentiment includes conjointly and in-separably all these three ideas—a *right*, *obligation*, and *sanction*. I am under certain *obligations* with regard to others—that is, others have a right to exact from me certain fulfilments and certain for-bearances, whether it may happen to suit my incli-nation, or not, to practise them.

I am possessed of certain *rights* in regard to others —that is, others are obliged to practise certain fulfilments and forbearances towards me, whether it may be agreeable to them or not. I am *obliged* towards others, and they are in like manner *obliged* towards me. I have certain *rights* in regard to others, and they on their parts have certain *rights* in regard to me. There is an indissoluble reciprocity of right and obligation—and that too assured by a common sanction. I feel that it does not depend upon my free-will whether I will perform or decline my obligations towards others, nor upon the free-will of others whether they perform or decline their obligations towards me. I feel as if both they and I were subject to a common superintending force, commanding both and restraining both, and capable of being invoked by either, in case of neglect or violation by the other, for purposes of compulsion or redress. In point of fact, there is no real extraneous force which fully and completely corresponds to the idea of this ethical *quasi-sanction*, though there are some real forces which go a certain way towards it, and suggest the lineaments of that idea which the fancy afterwards fills up. But it is not the less true that the idea of this quasi-sanction is an element in the common form of ethical sentiment, partly real, partly strengthened by our imagination for the purpose of guaranteeing the reciprocity of right and obligation —as a fancied *vinculum* between them.

If we suppose either the feeling of right without

that of obligation, or the feeling of obligation without that of right, in either case the ethical sentiment
will be broken up and deprived of its specific character.   The feeling of right without obligation, is
simple mastery or superiority : that of obligation
without right, is simple subjection.   Either of these
is radically distinct from ethical sentiment.   In fact
the latter has in it all the elements of a supposed
contract or covenant—if there had been a real
contract or covenant, the feeling would not have
been at all different.   Every separate individual feels
that he is bound to certain observances and certain
forbearances towards others and for the benefit of
others : but every one at the same time feels that
others are bound to certain observances and certain
forbearances towards him, and that the same sanction
which ensures the performance of this *quasi-covenant*,
from him to others, also ensures the like performance
from others to him.   On the one hand, each man is
a member of the society, entitled to exact from every
other member various performances and abstinences.
On the other hand, he is an individual agent acting
for himself, but bound to perform certain obligations
and to exhibit certain dispositions towards others.
These are in fact the two different phases of the same
ethical sentiment : whoever is not impressed with
both of them, cannot be said to be *ethically minded*.

Moralists seem often to speak of the sentiment of

ethical obligation as if it stood alone and unconnected with any sentiment of right. Looking at the matter with reference to practice, one can easily understand why they have done this: for every man is certain to set quite sufficient value on his own rights, but he is not equally certain to be sufficiently attentive to his obligations. But it is nevertheless an error to suppose that the sense of obligation stands alone: for the sense of right is indissolubly connected with it and forms an equally essential part of the ethical man. If I duly perform my obligations towards others—still more if I perform what is beyond my obligations—I acquire thereby a right to certain favourable sentiments and to conduct betokening such sentiments at the hands of others. If others do not accord to me such favourable sentiments, or do not requite me by the corresponding tenor of action, they are in the wrong—they do me wrong and they are wanting in the obligations incumbent upon *them*. By a certain line of conduct on my part, the esteem of others is acquired to me as of right, and they are obliged to accord it to me. Now this feeling, of an acquired right to the esteem of others, is inseparably interwoven with the sentiment of obligation, or with the idea of right doing on my part—just as the feeling, of a supervening liability to the disesteem of others, is interwoven with the idea of wrong doing or the violation of obligation. The consciousness of right to the esteem of others, is called *self-esteem*: the consciousness of liability to the disesteem of others, is called *self-reproach*. When we speak of the esteem of others, or of the disesteem of others, we mean of course such conduct on their part as betokens these sentiments: it is only by some overt manifestation that their sentiments can become known to us.

The desire of acquiring a right to the esteem of others and of avoiding the liability to their disesteem, is the genuine *ethical motive*—which, when assisted by the requisite knowledge and power, is quite sure to lead to right action. It is true that when the performance of obligation has become habitual, the virtuous man feels himself impelled by a rapid and vehement sentiment of which he does not stop to render any account. But it may be shewn incontrovertibly that the desire of obtaining the esteem of others, and the feeling of an acquired right to such esteem, make a part of the sentiment. For if it so happens that he fails to obtain that esteem, he suffers grief and disappointment, and labours under an indignant consciousness of having been wronged by others.

A man, who has been for years undeviatingly honest or veracious, if he finds himself mistrusted or suspected of dishonesty, will be acutely pained and will feel himself grievously wronged. He will be conscious that he has deserved esteem and confidence, and that he is entitled to complain of others for treating him otherwise. Now the existence of such feelings proves that both the desire to enjoy esteem and the consciousness of his eventual right to it, formed a main element at least in that habitual sentiment which impelled him to the observance of honesty and veracity.

The genuine ethical motive is,—the desire at all events of acquiring a right to the esteem of others, and if possible consistently with this, the desire of actually enjoying it—the desire of escaping conscious liability to the disesteem of others, and if possible consistently with this, the desire of escaping their actual disesteem. To a perfectly virtuous man, the consciousness that he deserves esteem will be more gratifying than the actual enjoyment of it — the consciousness of deserving disesteem will be more painful than the actual suffering of it—if he is reduced to choose between the two. The consciousness of a perfect title to the esteem and admiration of others, and the actual possession of it at the same time, is the ethical *summum bonum*; the consciousness of unequivocal liability to the disesteem and abhorrence of others, and the actual incurring of it at the same time, is the ethical *summum malum*; and the desire to obtain the one and avoid the other, constitutes the *ethical motive*. Regard to the esteem and re- proach of others, either as it is dispensed, or as it ought to be dispensed if others were right-minded. is the basis of virtuous action. If the actual public refuse to a virtuous man the esteem which he deserves, he feels that they do him *wrong,* and withhold from him what he has a *right to*—he persuades himself that the time will come when they will do him *justice*—and the idea of the imaginary public who coincide with him in judgment, outweighs in his mind the actual public who are opposed to him. The ethical sentiment, in all its forms and varieties, presents the idea of a public (meaning thereby persons other than the agent himself)—it presents them not merely as persons to whom the agent is bound, but as persons who are not less bound to him, under a certain common sanction. The ideas of *Merit —Demerit—Reward—Punishment—Right to esteem or respect—Liability to aversion or contempt*—all have reference to this public and to its anticipated judgment. *Wrong* is that which *deserves condemnation* or *punishment.*

When I say that obligation and right are correlative and mutually imply each other, I do not mean that every specific act which we perform under a sense of obligation must necessarily correspond to a specific right vested in some other determinate persons. In performing any particular obligatory act, the sentiment by which we are impelled is not one peculiar to that act alone, but common to

that act along with a great many others : and it
is that general sentiment of *ethical obligation* which
correlates and is indissolubly conjoined with the
general sentiment of *ethical right*; making up both
together, when joined by the ideal vinculum, called
a *sanction*, what is properly called *ethical sentiment*.
Ethical sentiment, then, consists of a cluster of ideas
and feelings indissolubly united together by association, in such manner that the occurrence of phenomena in real life, in a way conformable to this
association, occasions to us a feeling of satisfaction—
the occurrence of phenomena in a manner contrary
to it, creates a feeling of displeasure or indignation.
Restraints are to be submitted to, and services to be
performed, by each individual agent, as the indispensable condition, but at the same time as the
certain and constant cause, of similar restraints and
services, and (what is still more) of the continuance
of favourable dispositions and esteem on the part of
others.   It is upon these dispositions that the voluntary and ready performance of acts depends : and
the desire of favourable disposition on the part of
others, as the permanent cause of continued benefit
and protection to us, forms a much more important
feature in the ethical associations than the anticipation of any special and definite services.   In fact,
ethically speaking, an act is regarded more in respect to the evidence which it affords of the settled

disposition of the agent, than with a view to its own specific consequences. This forms one remarkable ground of discrepancy between the point of view of Ethics and the point of view of Law. The feeling above described is formed by associations begun at a very early age and continually repeated under circumstances of the greatest importance to our happiness. The elements of which it is composed become so intimately blended, and so rapid and vehement in their action upon our feelings, that we cannot detect them separately at the moment of passing. But that all these elements are really present, is shewn most incontestably when the sentiment comes to be deliberately unrolled. If I remonstrate with another person respecting some wrong which he has done—if I console him for wrong which he has suffered—if I discuss with him or dispute with him respecting wrong done by some third party—if I hearten him up to the discharge of some very painful duty—if I arbitrate or give sentence in any dispute—in all these cases the ethical sentiment has to be taken to pieces and the separate elements of it distinctly brought out and appealed to. The topics and arguments then insisted on, affect a man's reason because they revive what had previously passed in his mind, because he is conscious that they are embodied as elements in his ethical sentiment and because he is also aware that the latter sentiment has already undergone various modifications during his transition from infancy to manhood and may perhaps undergo still more in the future. If the sentiment were simple, uncompounded and instinctive, the topics which are now found more or less operative could have no bearing upon it.

You may call it a natural sentiment if you will— meaning thereby a sentiment which is formed by association, but which is quite certain to be formed more or less in every variety of human society. The foundations of the sentiment are doubtless laid in human nature; but the sentiment itself is composed of ideas and feelings gradually, and at last indissolubly, united together; the causes which determine such ideas and feelings to become associated together, being quite universal in their operation, and acting upon every individual (with certain modifications and varieties) who is brought up in anything like an established form of social relations. The ethical sentiment is *natural*, in the sense of *universal:* inasmuch as the formation of it depends upon causes of universal occurrence, not peculiar to any one age, or to any one form of society, or to any one particular mode of training. But it is not natural in the sense of simple, uncompounded and instinctive.

The earliest and rudest form in which the ethical sentiment presents itself, is when a child conceives

the kindness or unkindness of others towards him to
be conditioned on a certain mode of behaviour on
his part towards them.   Orders are issued which he
is required to obey : if he does not obey, painful
consequences follow : on the other hand, if he does
obey, he finds by experience that kindness and good
treatment on the part of others is the consequence,
and he learns to expect this with the full assurance
which ultimately ripens into a feeling of right.
Obligation to obey, as the necessary condition to
obtaining the kindness and good treatment of those
around : assurance of receiving that kindness, in
the event of obedience—this is the nascent state of
the ethical feeling, in the mind of a child.

If we consider the perfect and absolute helplessness of a child, we shall see that the aid of those
around is essential to every instant of his waking
existence — that reliance upon their aid must in-
evitably become the most familiar of all his ideas,
and the most constant of all his necessities. When
he feels a want, his only resource is to cry, in order
to bring some one to his assistance. The mere
thought, in so far as he is capable of conceiving it,
of being deprived of that aid, must be of all sentiments the most intolerably painful. That the desire
of the constant aid and protection of others should
become the most intense of all desires, and the fear
of their negation of aid the most insupportable of

all fears, is a natural consequence of the long helplessness of childhood.

As a child grows older, he perceives that the
granting or refusing of such aid by others depends
upon their dispositions towards him : and that these
dispositions on the part of others depend upon his
conduct towards them. The favourable dispositions
of others, and the symptoms and evidences of such
dispositions, become, by the common process of association, the object of his earnest attachment, as being
the ascertained and exclusive causes of everything
which is essential to his existence : but such dispositions are not to be obtained unless he obeys certain
orders given by those around; unless he refrains
from actions which they dislike, and manifests dispositions agreeable to them — while, on the other
hand, if he does obey the orders, refrain from the
forbidden actions, and manifest the dispositions
desired from him, the favourable dispositions of
others will most certainly be assured to him. Here,
then, is the first *genesis* of the ethical sentiment—the
idea and confident expectation of favourable dispositions on the part of others, as the assured consequence of one set of actions and dispositions on his
part—the idea and confident expectation of unfavourable dispositions on the part of others, as the assured
consequence of one set of actions and dispositions on
his part—the idea and confident expectation of un-

favourable dispositions on the part of others, as the assured consequence of another set of actions and dispositions on his part. Good or bad dispositions from others, conditional upon his own conduct or disposition towards others—is the constant type— the main and essential element of ethical feelings.

Having formed this association in his own case, a child easily makes the next step of applying a similar rule in judging of the relations of one person towards another. Good or bad dispositions on the part of others towards A, conditional upon the conduct or disposition of A towards others—this is a rule which he will readily follow out and apply to every individual successively. And this is the idea of obligation and right.—The persons towards whom a child first learns to conceive this sentiment of obligation are adult persons, in the first place immeasurably superior to himself in power, in the next place generally full of active fondness and affection towards him. The consciousness of inferiority and feebleness is blended with all the sentiments of infancy: a child feels that he has not the slenderest power of acting upon the fears of others, but he feels at the same time that he has great power of acting upon their love and fondness. Hence he looks upon the goodwill and affection of persons around him as consequences which he expects to ensue from certain conduct on his own part, but which at the same time he has not the means of enforcing, if withheld, however the negation of them may displease him. But in process of time his own sense of power increases with his growth, and he also sees instances of the exercise of power by one man over another, so as to appreciate comparative superiority and inferiority in the individuals around him. From these circumstances arise the rudiments of the idea called *sanction*, or of a certain compulsory force which may be employed to procure for him those advantages which he conceives as belonging to his own good conduct, in the event of their not being freely conceded. Advantages so capable of being secured are conceived as *rights*, in the fullest sense—expectations of benefit which if not realized by the free-will of the party at whose hands they are expected, are supposed to be enforceable by authority or superior power of some kind.

It would seem, therefore, that in the mind of a child, the idea of *ethical obligation* arises earlier than that of *ethical right*—meaning by ethical obligation the idea of beneficent dispositions and conduct from others in consequence exclusively of certain conduct of his own. Though he would be painfully disappointed if the consequences which he thus expects were withheld, yet it can hardly be said that he fancied himself to have a *right* to them, until he conceived the idea of some possible means of enforcing them. This in fact is the sentiment entertained of obligation towards some very great and at the same time very much venerated power—the paternal power, or still more the divine power. To the eye of a child, the power of his father seems omnipotence : he learns to feel ethical obligation towards his father, but he has at first no sense of ethical right over him. Filial obligation in its purest and earliest form is ethical obligation without any sense of ethical right.

But when the child has so far grown up as to feel a certain force of his own, and so far enlarged his experience as to be cognizant of the various powers around him, he acquires the idea of a common sanction to enforce obligations and prevent wrong, as well on the part of others towards him, as on his part towards others. This common sanction is usually the authority of the head of the family over the members. This is the first state of things of which a child acquires experience—various members of a family living under the common authority of the head or father. To that authority he pays obedience and from that authority he receives protection. It is employed to compel him to behave in a certain way towards others, and to refrain from hurting them. The ideas of obedience and protection thus come to be conceived as depending upon a common sanction and to be indissolubly associated together in his mind. The extraneous authority on which alone he has to rely for protection, will not be exerted in his defence unless upon condition of certain acts and abstinences and dispositions on his part: and *vice versâ*, if he performs these acts, &c. he may confidently rely upon such authority being exerted for his security. This confident, but conditional, reliance, constitutes the feeling of *ethical right*: the disappointment of that feeling is the sense of being *wronged*. Negation of favour—censure—or punishment from the common authority to himself, in the event of his doing forbidden acts or neglecting to do enjoined acts: similar negation of favour—similar censure—similar punishment—from the same authority, towards others, in the event of *their* doing forbidden acts, or neglecting to do enjoined acts, towards him.

III.

Having traced the sources of ethical sentiment to the self-regarding tendencies of our nature, it now remains to trace also the operation of the principle of sympathy on the first conception of the notion and the feeling of a common interest and common liabilities with others; and to shew how the pleasures and pains of others, conceived conjointly with our own and conceived as arising from the same causes with our own, come to affect our minds so forcibly and vividly. Those persons, who are the causes of harm and suffering to ourselves conjointly with others, become thus the objects of our terror and aversion; those who are the causes of protection and benefit to ourselves in conjunction with others, become the objects of our attachment and gratitude. Each of these feelings, by being shared with others, is greatly intensified and prolonged: each is also modified in its nature by being divested of what is exclusive and personal to ourselves: each appears, in consequence of being shared by all around us, to be based on a foundation of reason and extraneous authority independent of any individual impulse— Φήμη—Θεός τις καὶ αὐτή.

When this feeling of a common interest with others has once acquired a footing in our minds, together with the sentiments emanating from it, of joint attachment to the common benefactor—joint aversion to the common enemy—it farther becomes an idea highly painful to every one to imagine himself the object of this joint aversion, and an idea highly pleasurable to imagine himself the object of this joint attachment.

We are thus brought by a second and a different road to the same end—that of strongly desiring the favourable sentiment of those around us; and shrinking with apprehension from their unfavourable sentiment. The absolute necessity in which we are placed, even for our own protection and comfort, of conciliating the former, and avoiding the latter, is one road—the sympathy which we feel in their pains and pleasures, and the conception thence arising of a common interest with them, is another road—each conducting to the same conclusion—each tending to render the favourable sentiments of others among the objects of our most anxious desires, and the unfavourable sentiments of others a source to us of the liveliest fear and suffering.

We also arrive by means of sympathy, and by means of that feeling of a common interest which sympathy inspires, at the sentiment of *approbation* and *disapprobation*—sentiments which are always conceived as belonging to us in common with a number of others.

But we do not arrive, by means of sympathy alone, at the feeling of right or obligation, or the idea of a sanction binding them together. Right and obligation are founded upon the self-regarding tendencies, not upon the sympathetic tendencies, of our nature —they assume a pre-existing antithesis between each man and his fellows, each having a separate object, his own individual happiness, to take care of. They are introduced for the purpose of regulating this discrepancy—of reconciling the discrepant parties in an ascertained common medium—of limiting the extent to which, and the means by which, each man may pursue his own separate happiness, and of defining the terms on which he may make sure of obtaining the forbearance and co-operation of every other man.

When it is said that I am *under obligation* to act in a certain manner, a constraining force is implied as acting upon me : it is assumed, that my own uncontrolled inclinations might lead me otherwise—the necessity of constraint is founded upon my having self-regarding tendencies.   On the other hand, when I affirm that I have a *certain right*, a constraining force is implied as acting upon others—it is assumed that others have self-regarding tendencies, which might induce them to withhold or to resist the benefit to which my right relates.   Both right and obligation are founded upon the supposition that each man has separate and divergent inclinations of his own—a sort of centrifugal tendency : they regulate and modify these inclinations, in order that they may be brought into a certain degree of harmony in the members of the society generally.

Though the notion and the feelings of right and obligation are originally based upon the self-regarding tendencies of our nature, yet when once developed fully in the mind, they become social and comprehensive in the highest degree.   They are recognised and venerated as the grand source of security not merely to ourselves, but also to every other member of the society. They are in fact more extensively social even than the principle of sympathy—for sympathy cannot reach very powerfully beyond a limited number of persons, whereas a deep felt sense of right and obligation may pervade the whole of a very large community.

From the self-regarding tendencies of each individual, and from the belief, in each, of the like self-regarding tendencies in others, are derived the notions and the feelings of *right* and *wrong*, obligatory or forbidden — and our distinction between various agents according as they are disposed to act *rightly* or *wrongly*, in a manner *obligatory* or *forbidden*, &c. From the sympathetic tendencies of each individual and from his belief of the like sympathetic tendencies in others, we derive the notions and the feelings of what is good and bad (the cause of relief and comfort, or of pain and uneasiness) not to ourselves singly and exclusively, but to ourselves in conjunction with others—good and bad for *all*, or good and bad absolutely : and also our distinction of agents according as they do what is good or what is bad.

These two feelings, though derived from different sources and each modifying the other more or less, are generally found in harmony, occasionally in conflict. Generally speaking, what is *bad*, is regarded as wrong, though what is wrong is not always regarded as bad—*i.e.* it does not always painfully affect our benevolent sympathies. A man who, in order to accomplish a particular work of benevolence, departs from the strict obligation of justice, will be generally considered as having acted wrongly—but he will not be treated by most persons as having done a bad act —still less as being himself a bad agent.

A man who does a wrong act with a benevolent view is looked upon, by ordinary persons, as deserving of very little censure, and very considerable indulgence. It most frequently occurs, however, that wrong acts are not done with a benevolent view— the *wrong* act is generally a *bad* act—the benevolent impulses do in the greater number of cases coincide with dictates of justice.

The words good and bad are by no means constantly used to signify benevolent and malevolent agents : but I think they most commonly tend to that meaning—a kindly or an unkindly disposition.

Benevolence is in point of fact, in itself, an undistinguishing impulse, which requires to be governed and regulated, like our other impulses and affections, of the self-regarding kind. Anger, fear, gratitude, desire of money, desire of power, appetites of every kind, all require a certain restraining and guiding authority—all are to be indulged only so far as consists with some definite and approved end.

It is the *ethical sentiment* which furnishes this

restraining and guiding authority for all of them. In its rudest state, as it is felt in the mind of an untaught and unreflecting man, this sentiment is only an obedience to the actual judgment of those around him, such as he knows by experience that they are likely to pronounce, and such as he would himself concur in pronouncing with regard to any other agent.

In the rationalized state of *ethical sentiment*, where a man has by reflection formed to himself the idea of a standard more exalted than that of the persons around him, he often appeals to their judgment as it ought to be, rather than as it actually is—to their judgment as it would be if they were raised to his level of instruction.

In every person above the age of absolute childhood, ethical sentiment involves more or less of a judgment of reason, the result of comparison and reflection upon the phenomena which have passed within our experience. A child has found himself punished or rewarded—frowned upon or caressed— under circumstances in which he did not anticipate it: he has been witness to many expressions of opinion and many instances of retributory behaviour on the part of others, which have greatly astonished him: he has heard disputes and contradiction between the persons around him, in regard to what is right or wrong—all these phenomena make impressions upon him, sometimes very strong impressions; they stimulate his reasoning powers, to endeavour to bring what is confused and disorderly into something like system and regularity : he has to follow out a number of different analogies, to strike a balance between such as conflict with each other, and to extract out of the whole an intelligible rule for his own guidance. He finds himself prompted by different impulses in particular cases, and reduced to the necessity of choosing between them—he finds himself in doubt as to the various rules or orders which have been issued to him by those whom he respects and which are not always in harmony with each other, so that he cannot at the same time obey all of them—and he is thus reduced to the necessity of employing his intellectual powers, in order to rescue himself from a state of painful embarrassment. Though the general ethical sentiment is early implanted by association in the mind, yet the applications of this sentiment to particular cases are constantly liable to involve a process of reason—nor can the sentiment be brought to bear upon our conduct without this process. Ethical sentiment properly so called is not feeling *alone*, like benevolence, compassion, paternal or filial love, sexual impulse, anger, fear, &c.—it is a *rationalized sentiment*—a process of feeling and reason combined.

Every young person on coming into the world

finds the ethical sentiments of the society ready
formed and in active operations. He embraces, by a
process of association which passes almost unconsciously to himself, those sentiments which he finds
entertained by the persons around him ; he begins by
obeying directions given by those who have the command of his happiness and comforts, and who manifest tender affections towards him. He does not at
first perceive any meaning or recognise any advantage in the orders given : he obeys them because
they are issued by those whom he loves as the causes
of all his pleasure, and of whom he stands in need as
his sole protectors against all his pains and wants.
His first ideas of what it is *right* or *wrong* to do, are
derived from the orders and prohibitions of these
superiors : the former word and the actions to which
it is applied are associated with the affectionate dispositions and willing aid of those upon whom he
depends, the latter word and the actions on which it
is bestowed, with the contrary sentiment—and they
thus carry with them the feelings belonging to love,
veneration, and sense of entire dependence. He
learns to view circumstances, and to estimate individual characters and pretensions, in the same
manner as those by whom he is surrounded. This is
indeed a gradual process, including multiplied repe-
titions of separate acts of feeling and judgment, the
general result of which remains in the mind as a

permanent sentiment or disposition, but which are themselves individually forgotten and can never be recalled. Mr. Edgworth in his Practical Education (vol. i. ch. ix. p. 295, 3rd edit.) observes very justly : " The words right or wrong, and permitted or forbidden, are synonymous at first in the apprehensions of children : and obedience and disobedience are their only ideas of virtue and vice. Whatever we command to be done, or rather whatever we associate with pleasure, they imagine to be *right :* whatever we prohibit, provided we have uniformly associated it with pain, they believe to be *wrong.*" As their experience and instruction extends, they gradually acquire more enlarged notions of right and wrong, but the first form of the sentiment is of that which is enjoined, permitted or forbidden, by the authority on which he depends. The earliest form of moral sentiment thus includes the triple element of right, obligation, and sanction—a common presiding power which will restrain others from hurting him and restrain him from hurting others.

The persons with whom a child first lives, are the members of his own family, between whom and himself strong sympathies and mutual affection prevail. These feelings are mingled with his sentiments of right, wrong, and obligation, as regards the members of his own family ; so that the latter sentiments, during that early age, can scarcely be said to present themselves distinctly and in a separate state : they are at any rate greatly modified. But as a child grows up, he finds himself called upon to deal with persons with whom he has no pre-established sympathies, and who have no pre-established sympathies with him. At the same time his feeling of his own power, as compared with others, is greatly increased. He has less to hope from the pre-existing affection of those with whom he is now placed—but he has more to expect from the sentiment with which his own conduct may inspire them—from the gratitude, the hopes, and the fears, which they may entertain towards him. The treatment which he meets with from the persons with whom he never lives, depends more on his own behaviour than it did when he lived with his own family. There is no tenderness to excuse or disguise his faults—there is no inclination on the part of others to forestall his wants—there is no association of fondness on his part with the person in whom authority resides. The sentiment of obligation to be performed by him towards others and by others towards him, now presents itself distinctly and nakedly—or at least much less connected with affection and sympathy than when he was a child : for the feeling of sympathy with others, and still more the feeling of a common interest arising out of sympathy, is always existing and always producing a certain effect, although an effect much less than it did produce during the period of childhood. When the child grows up to be a man, he becomes what is called a responsible agent: the conduct of others towards him is for the most part determined by his conduct towards them: he is admitted to share in the general sympathy and in the general feeling of a common interest entertained by every individual around him, but he is not allowed to calculate upon any peculiar indulgence or favour. The less he can calculate upon the established affection of those around him, the more important it becomes to him to acquire their esteem : indeed without a certain measure of good feeling and esteem from those with whom he lives, life would become positively insupportable. Such fulfilments and forbearances as are necessary to purchase this minimum of esteem, *must* be performed, let the sacrifice be what it may. The painful associations connected with the loss of this minimum of good feeling on the part of others, are more intense and more effective than the pain of almost any degree of self-denial in other respects.

What sort of conduct on his part will be required of a man in order to purchase that degree of good feeling from others which is essential to his comfort —will be determined in a great degree by the station which he occupies in society. If he be a person of rank and wealth, less will be required from him in the way of *obligation*, and more will be

granted to him in the way of *right*: if he be a
person poor and of low degree, these proportions
will be reversed. And if he happens to be a slave,
the absolute property of one individual master, he is
altogether out of the pale of ethical sentiment: the
society neither ensure to him any rights, nor exact
from him any obligations; he is in a state of obligation to a master, whom he may love or hate,
according as he is treated, but in neither case is
the sentiment which animates him of an ethical
character.

The ancient poets have various striking passages
expressive of the incapacity of a slave for ethical
feeling—῞Ημισυ γὰρ τ᾽ ἀρετῆς ἄπο αἴνυται, &c. ῾Υγιὲς
οὐδὲν ψυχῆς δούλης—(Plato). Οὔποτε δουλείη κεφαλὴ
εὐθεῖα πέφυκεν—(Theognis). This fact would be
singly sufficient to shew that the ethical sentiment is the offspring of those relations in which a
man is placed to the society round him—that it is
not *natural* in the sense of *ready-made*, original, or
instinctive—but that it is a complex feeling, the
gradual result of associations which do not arise
except where a man is placed in certain relations
towards his fellows.

The esteem in which a man is held by his fellows
does not depend wholly and exclusively upon what
they may believe respecting his disposition, which is
strictly and properly the ethical measure. A very

poor and weak man, although his disposition may be the best possible, will obtain little esteem, and will be the object of hardly any sentiment except indifference or perhaps compassion. Whatever his disposition may be, his power of doing good or harm is too insignificant to excite any marked feeling.

The esteem in which a man is held depends partly on his dispositions, but partly also upon his power and resources of every kind, natural as well as acquired — partly too upon the accidental circumstances in which he has been placed, or particular associations which have become connected with his name and person.

A man desires to have full credit among his fellows for all the powers and resources which he possesses, as well as for the good mental dispositions which belong to him. To rob a man of the credit due to him from the former source, is an insult of the same sort as to deprive him of the credit due from the latter.

To be reproached with weakness, impotence, unfitness for the duties incumbent upon a man, ignorance of those accomplishments which are common with men of good condition, want of virile power, bastardy, ugliness, infamy of one's family, &c.—is an imputation quite as terrible and cutting as that of any ethical fault, such as dishonesty, mendacity,

injustice, cruelty, or ingratitude. The words *knave*,
rascal, *villain*, &c., originally meant persons of low
and mean condition : they have gradually come to
mean persons of bad moral character. The reproach
of Euryalus to Ulysses (Odyss. VIII.) that he is no
ἀθλητής, but nothing better than a ship-master, is
more warmly resented than almost any other
reproach in the poem. The loss of station, power,
consequence, &c., is painful in the same manner and
from the same causes as the loss of ethical merit—
both the one and the other deprive us of what we
feel to be a title to the esteem of the community
around. For a man who has been accustomed to a
high and commanding station, it is intolerable to live
in a low condition, even though there be no discomfort or positive suffering attending it. The conception of the altered esteem of others towards him
is always present to his mind, though he may perhaps experience no actual manifestations of such
alteration. The most acutely painful of all sentiments from others towards us, is that of contempt—
let it be even an indulgent contempt.

If we take the case of Œdipus, there is no
moral guilt (at least according to the ancient ideas)
which he has incurred. But he has involuntarily
and unconsciously committed acts which are objects
of horror to all around him, and he knows that
he has thus become odious to every one. The con-

sciousness of this feeling renders life insupportable to him.

The idea of that which other persons are thinking or feeling with respect to his character, position, station, and behaviour—is constantly present to every man's mind. He desires intensely that others should think highly of him in all these respects— that they should regard with esteem and favour his personal dispositions, his power, his station, and his pursuits. He dreads with equal intensity that others should think ill of him in these respects—that they should regard with odium or contempt his personal character, his power, his station, or his pursuits. Those acts of his own which will procure for him the former class of sentiments from others, he comes to contemplate with satisfaction and delight as respects the past and with desire of repetition as respects the future. Those acts of his own which will draw upon him the latter class of sentiments, he comes to contemplate with aversion as respects the past and with resolution to avoid as respects the future. The acts themselves become ultimately by the process of association, the object of a sentiment of their own, and are shunned or coveted for their own sake, the end, which originally caused them to be so, being no longer distinctly thought of or attended to.

That this is the real genesis of ethical sentiment in every individual mind, may be shewn by the analogy of other sentiments not ethical. There are in every society acts which are regarded as degrading and unsuitable to men in particular stations, though perhaps not at all discreditable to other persons—at any rate not involving any moral guilt, and therefore such as cannot be pretended to be the object of the supposed moral instinct. Now these degrading and unbecoming acts come to be regarded with aversion and shunned, in the same manner and from the same cause as immoral acts are shunned. A man shrinks from doing what is degrading and unbecoming, just as he shrinks from the idea of doing what is immoral: he is no more conscious of a distinct reference to the opinion of others in the one case than in the other : the sentiment which deters him from the one, appears just as immediate, as rapid, and as completely identified with the act itself, in the former as in the latter. The sentiment called *honour* in the mind of a gentleman is indisputably acquired by position and education, and is felt only by those who have been peculiarly placed and peculiarly educated : it enjoins him to do certain acts and to refrain from others, and it does so without any special or conscious allusion to those feelings on the part of others in which it originally took its rise. The first form which the sentiment of honour assumes is—" I must do this, for if I do not, I shall be thought dishonourable ; I must refrain from doing that, for if I do it, I shall be thought dishonourable." But the subsequent and mature form of the sentiment is different, after the association between the act and the idea of those feelings with which others regard the act, has become habitual and instantaneous. The sentiment then runs — "Such an act is an honourable act, therefore it must be done: such another act is a dishonourable act, therefore it must not be done." By the universal law of association, it is certain that this change in the nature and character of the sentiment will take place—that elements of thought and feeling which were originally distinctly impressed upon the mind, will come to be effaced from our consciousness as subjects of separate attention, after they have often passed through our minds in habitual and rapid conjunction.

Now the case is the same with the ethical sentiment as with the sentiment of honour: both are originally founded on our regard to the feelings which others may entertain towards us; both become in process of time and by the natural tendency of association, divested to a great degree of all conscious reference to those feelings. The difference no doubt is, that the sentiment of honour belongs more especially to a select class in the community, whereas ethical sentiment is founded on relations and necessity pervading all society, and is absolutely essential to bind together all those who live in any sort of communion. But as to the mode of generation, and the gradual change which the feeling undergoes by association, the analogy between the two is perfect.

If we were even to admit, as Dugald Stewart contends, that there is a moral instinct which leads us directly to consider certain acts as right, and certain other acts as wrong, without any reference to what others think or feel about them—it would still be impossible to ascribe any necessary correctness or authority to this supposed instinct. For no one can deny that the instinct not only may be, but constantly is, depraved and perverted : and if this be the case, it is on the same footing with other appetites and inclinations, requiring to be kept right by the supervision and control of reason.

It has been above stated that a child first derives his ethical sentiment from his experience of the feelings of others, and from the absolute necessity which keeps the feelings of others constantly present to his mind as causes of all his comforts and most of his sufferings. If the feelings of others were always uniform and consistent, it is probable that the ethical sentiment which a child would contract would be never combined with any operations of reason. But the feelings and opinions of others as to what is right and wrong are not always either harmonious or consistent : differences of opinion arise among individuals as to what is right or wrong, nor is the same individual always consistent with himself in his judgments on the matter : actions are considered wrong in one man when they are not wrong in another. A young person who grows up under such appearances, is perplexed by the dissentient judgments which he hears from different individuals, and is forced to employ his reason in order to reconcile them. By successive comparisons and reflections, he forms what is called a *standard* of his *own*, of right or wrong—of what is becoming or degrading in his position—of what is in good taste or in bad taste. It commonly happens, that he prefers the judgment of one section of those around him to that of the rest —from reverence for their authority, or personal affection, or any other cause. But this judgment which arises in his mind and which is called a *standard of his own*, as it is deduced from his own observation, comparisons, and reflections on what the opinions of others actually are, so it has when formed an essential and constant reference to the opinions of others *as they ought to be* ; or as he thinks they would be, if others were wise and right-minded. The idea of this imaginary public, wise and right-minded, is present to his mind as approving of the standard which he has adopted. His own approbation is only another expression for the approbation of this better and superior public. In common parlance, we often speak of a man's own standard as opposed to that of the persons around him : but if we analyse the sentiment described by the first form of words, it will appear to point distinctly at the idea which the agent entertains of the feelings of supposed persons other than himself. By acting up to his own standard of right and wrong, he feels that he acquires a title to the esteem of others : if they withhold it from him, it is their fault, and they are in the wrong : he has the sentiment *of good desert*, though others may not acknowledge it. He loves to do, and does do, that which he thinks *praiseworthy*, although he may foreknow that it will not be actually praised by those around him ; he hates to do, and does not do, that which he thinks *blameworthy*, although it may not be actually blamed by those whom he sees or hears. It is undeniable that in a certain number of minds the attachment to what they think *praiseworthy* overpowers their desire *of actual praise* ; and their repugnance to what they think *blameworthy*, surpasses their aversion to *actual* blame. But the attachment to that which is praiseworthy presupposes the attachment to actual praise —a man would never learn to esteem or value that which is praiseworthy if he had not previously delighted in and desired actual praise. In like manner the aversion to what is blameworthy presupposes the aversion to actual blame : no man would ever come

to dread or to shun that which is blameworthy, if
he had not previously endured acute pangs from the
bearing of actual blame. The idea of what is praiseworthy is derived by a secondary process of association from that which is actually praised : the idea of
the blameworthy, in like manner, from that which
is actually blamed. The fundamental idea of the
whole, is that of the kindness and good feeling and
esteem of others as an acquisition of primary necessity, indispensable to our comfort; that of the
unkindness, hatred and disesteem of others, as the
cause of pain, loss, and suffering of the most terrible
amount. From this association all virtue, even in
its greatest refinement and improvement, deduces its
origin.

The judgment of others, such as an individual
actually sees or hears it pronounced upon himself or
upon his own conduct, very often differs seriously from
the judgment of others as he conceives it. First, the
individual himself knows much more than any one
else can possibly know, respecting his own conduct
and motives and disposition. What is called his *own
judgment of himself*, is the idea which he forms of the
judgment of others as it would be if they possessed
the same fulness of knowledge, and contemplated the
matter with the same intensity of interest, as he does
himself. But this is a supposition never actually
realized : others never know so much about his con-

duct and intentions as he himself does, nor do they feel sufficient anxiety respecting it to take any great pains about enlightening themselves. Their sentiments may often be intense and violent, but it is seldom combined with any earnest research into the less obvious parts of the case, and never founded upon complete knowledge or accurate appreciation of all the influential circumstances. But the ideal spectator without, as the agent conceives him, is a person supposed to possess entire knowledge of all the circumstances, and a judgment intent and concentrated upon the case : he is a critic such as the persons without actually would be, if they could follow all the workings of the agent's mind from first to last ; he is on a par with the actual public, and differing from the agent, in so far as concerns his impartiality—he is on a par with the agent himself, and differing from the actual public, only so far as respects the completeness of his knowledge. In every young man's mind, this notion of ideal spectators more enlightened than the actual spectators, or of the actual spectators as they would be if they were more enlightened, is quite certain to be formed and to exercise more or less of influence, because no man can altogether banish the supposition that others know that which is familiar to himself and to his own thoughts. The judgment of these ideal spectators may often be altogether at variance with that of the

actual spectators by whom the agent is surrounded:
the supposed favourable judgment of the former
may be more gratifying to him, and their supposed
unfavourable judgment more afflicting, than the
actual criticism, favourable or unfavourable, which
he hears pronounced by the latter.

This appeal to the ideal spectators, thoroughly
well informed and enlightened, is what constitutes
the sense of *good or ill desert,* or merit and demerit.
That estimation which I suppose myself to deserve—
and that estimation which I suppose that a right-
minded and well-informed spectator would accord to
me—are only two modes of expressing the same
thing. If the actual spectators around do not accord
to me this estimation, I regard them either as not
right-minded or as not well-informed—I constitute
myself their censor, instead of recognising them as
mine.

There are two grounds on which an individual
agent may appeal from the judgment of the actual
spectators around him. Either he may say that they
do not know all the circumstances of the case : or he
may say that they do not judge and feel rightly—
that they condemn or approve behaviour which a
perfectly wise man would not condemn or approve.
He may appeal either on grounds of fact or on
grounds of law.

I have already remarked that every agent unavoidably comes to form the conception of some spectators better informed as to matters of fact than the actual spectators are. He transfers his own knowledge of fact to the bosoms of the spectators. By a similar process, he arrives at the conception of a public judging upon different principles (better or worse, as the case may be) from the real public by whom he is surrounded. He invests them to a certain extent not only with his own knowledge of fact, but with his own mode of view—not brought out ready made by any original and inexplicable instinct, but formed by gradual process of reasoning or comparison out of what he has seen and heard and experienced. The differences of sentiment amongst different people round him with respect to what is right or wrong, proper or improper, suitable or unsuitable—render it necessary for him to take one side or the other in such disputes. He is sure to find himself at variance with one portion or other of the community around him upon this subject, and he thus learns to consider himself in the light of a person having ethical views of his own. Each successive ethical judgment, which he has heard, or seen, or been made to feel, from his earliest recollection, produces a certain impression upon his mind : the state of his ethical sentiment as it exists in him at any given moment is the result of all these previous impressions—more or less compared, combined, or contrasted, according to the

measure of his intellect. In the general cast of
ethical sentiment, all the members of the same community come near to agreement : in the applications
of detail, there are wide differences, and each individual acquires a certain independent view of his
own. In one man's mind, acts and dispositions of
one kind will come to be associated with the idea of
the esteem and disesteem of others ; in another man's
mind, acts and dispositions of another kind.

From this general harmony, disturbed by particular differences, in the ethical sentiment of various
individuals, there arises in the mind of each man
an indistinct conception of a standard of morality
common to all of them, and some sort of desire to
ascertain what that standard is. The arguments by
which any dispute with respect to the right or wrong
in a particular case is conducted, imply a persuasion
in the disputants that there is some common principle
which ought to serve as a basis of reasoning to both
of them. It is true that this conception of a common
standard is faint and undeveloped : with ordinary
persons, it is never distinctly made a subject of research, and therefore is very unlikely to be discovered : moreover the prosecution of the enquiry
demands intellectual efforts and patient attention
such as very few persons can give. But still the
rudiments of such an idea—the divination of it, as it
were—are in every one's mind : arguments which

allude to it and suppose its existence are urged by every one and admitted by every one.

Every man knows that there is a better and a worse in the ethical sentiments of different individuals : every man is conscious that he has himself undergone improvement in this respect, and that his own ethical sentiment has changed for the better as compared with what it once was, nor will he hesitate to admit that there is room for still farther improvement, and that there are persons around him who already stand higher in this respect than himself. This belief and aspiration after a common standard not yet distinctly ascertained is one of the many separate elements constituting ethical sentiment.

Ethical obligation means subjection to the sanction of society, and the manifestation of such conduct as that sanction enjoins. Ethical right is a reliance on that same sanction, to be employed in our favour, and on a certain behaviour towards us on the part of other individuals, conformable to its injunctions.

ESSAY V.

THE ETHICS OF ARISTOTLE.

THE ETHICS OF ARISTOTLE.

I.

THE Ethics of Aristotle presuppose certain conditions in the persons to whom they are addressed, without which they cannot be read with profit. They presuppose a certain training, both moral and intellectual, in the pupil.

First, the reason of the pupil must be so far developed, as that he shall be capable of conceiving the idea of a scheme of life and action, and of regulating his momentary impulses more or less by a reference to this standard. He must not live by passion, obeying without reflection the appetite of the moment, and thinking only of grasping at this immediate satisfaction. The habit must have been formed of referring each separate desire to some rational measure, and of acting or refraining to act according as such a comparison may dictate.

Next, a certain experience must have been acquired concerning human affairs, and concerning the actions of men with their causes and consequences. Upon these topics all the reasonings and all the illustrations contained in every theory of Ethics must

necessarily turn : so that a person thoroughly inex-
perienced would be incompetent to understand them.

For both these two reasons, no youthful person,
nor any person of mature years whose mind is still
tainted with the defects of youth, can be a competent
learner of Ethics or Politics (Eth. Nic. i. 7. Compare vii. 8). Such a pupil will neither appreciate
the reasonings, nor obey the precepts (i. 3).

Again, a person cannot receive instruction in
Ethics with advantage unless he has been subjected
to a good practical discipline, so as to have acquired
habits of virtuous action, and to have been taught to
feel pleasure and pain on becoming occasions and in
reference to becoming objects. Unless the circumstances by which he has been surrounded and the
treatment which he has received, have been such as
to implant in him a certain vein of sentiment and to
give a certain direction to his factitious pleasures and
pains—unless obedience to right precepts has to a
certain degree been made habitual with him—he will
not be able to imbibe, still less to become attached to,
even the *principia* of ethical reasoning (Eth. Nic. i.
4. 7). The well-trained man, who has already
acquired virtuous habits, has within himself the ἀρχὴ,
or beginning, from which happiness proceeds : he
may do very well, even though the reason on which
these habits were formed should never become known
to him : but he will at least readily apprehend and

understand the reason when it is announced. The ἀρχαὶ or beginnings to which ethical philosophy points and from whence the conduct which it enjoins is derived, are obtained only by habituation, not by induction nor by perception, like other ἀρχαί: and we ought in all our investigations to look after the ἀρχὴ in the way which the special nature of the subject requires, and to be very careful to define it well (i. 4, i. 7).

In considering Aristotle's doctrine respecting the ἀρχαὶ of ethical and political science, and the way in which they are to be discovered and made available, we should keep in mind that he announces the end and object of these sciences to be, not merely the enlargement of human knowledge, but the determination of human conduct towards certain objects: not theory, but practice: not to teach us what virtue is, but to induce us to practise it—" Since then the present science is not concerned with speculation, *like the others*. For here we enquire, not in order that we may know what virtue is, but in order that we may become good, otherwise there would be no profit in the enquiry " (ii. 2. *See* also i. 2, i. 5, vi. 5).

The remarks which Aristotle makes about the different ways of finding out and arriving at ἀρχαὶ, are curious. Some principles or beginnings are obtained by *induction*—others by *perception*—others by habituation in a certain way—others again in other

ways.   Other modes of arriving at ἀρχαὶ are noticed
by the philosopher himself in other places.   For
example, the ἀρχαὶ of demonstrative science are said
to be discovered by intellect (νοῦς)—vi. 6–7.   There
is a passage however in vi. 8 in which he seems to
say that the ἀρχαὶ of the wise man (σόφος) and the
natural man (φυσικὸς) are derived from experience:
which I find it difficult to reconcile with the preceding chapters, where he calls wisdom a compound
of intellect and science (ἐπιστήμη), and where he
gives Thales and Anaxagoras as specimens of wise
men.   By vi. 6—it seems that wisdom has reference
to matters of demonstrative science : how then can it
be true that a youth may be a mathematician without
being a wise man ?

Moreover, Aristotle takes much pains, at the commencement of his treatise on Ethics, to set forth the
inherent intricacy and obscurity of the subject, and
to induce the reader to be satisfied with conclusions
not absolutely demonstrative.   He repeats this observation several times — a sufficient proof that the
evidence for his own opinions did not appear to himself altogether satisfactory (Eth. Nic. i. 3, i. 7,
ii. 2).   The completeness of the proof (he says)
must be determined by the subject-matter : a man of
cultivated mind will not ask for better proof than
the nature of the case admits: and human action, to
which all ethical theory relates, is essentially fluc-

tuating and uncertain in its consequences, so that every general proposition which can be affirmed or denied concerning it, is subject to more or less of exception. If this degree of uncertainty attaches even to general reasonings on ethical subjects, the particular applications of these reasonings are still more open to mistake: the agent must always determine for himself at the moment, according to the circumstances of the case, without the possibility of sheltering himself under technical rules of universal application: just as the physician or the pilot is obliged to do in the course of his profession. " Now the actions and the interests of men exhibit no fixed rule, just like the conditions of health. And if this is the case with the universal theory, still more does the theory that refers to particular acts present nothing that can be accurately fixed; for it falls not under any art or any system, but the actors themselves must always consider what suits the occasion, just as happens in the physician's and the pilot's art. But though this is the case with the theory at present, *we must try to give it some assistance*" ($\pi\epsilon\iota\rho\alpha\tau\acute{\epsilon}o\nu$ $\beta o\eta\theta\epsilon\hat{\iota}\nu$).—Eth. Nic. 2.

The last words cited are remarkable. They seem to indicate, that Aristotle regarded the successful prosecution of ethical enquiries as all but desperate. He had previously said (i. 3)—" There is so much difference of opinion and so much error respecting what is honourable and just, of which political science treats, that these properties of human action seem to exist merely by positive legal appointment, and not by nature. And there is the same sort of error respecting what things are good, because many persons have sustained injury from them, some having already been brought to destruction through their wealth, others through their courage."

One cannot but remark how entirely this is at variance with the notion of a moral sense or instinct, or an intuitive knowledge of what is right and wrong. Aristotle most truly observes that the details of our daily behaviour are subject to such an infinite variety of modifications, that no pre-established rules can be delivered to guide them : we must act with reference to the occasion and the circumstances. Some few rules may indeed be laid down, admitting of very few exceptions : but the vast majority of our proceedings cannot be subjected to any rule whatever, except to the grand and all-comprehensive rule, if we are indeed so to call it, of conforming to the ultimate standard of morality.

Supposing the conditions above indicated to be realized—supposing a certain degree of experience in human affairs, of rational self-government, and of habitual obedience to good rules of action, to be already established in the pupil's mind, the theory of ethics may then be unfolded to him with great advantage (i. 3). It is not meant to be implied that a man must have previously acquired the perfection of practical reason and virtue before he acquaints himself with ethical theory; but he must have proceeded a certain way towards the acquisition.

Ethics, as Aristotle conceives them, are a science closely analogous to if not a subordinate branch of Politics. (I do not however think that he employs the word Ἠθικὴ in the same distinct and substantive meaning as πολιτικὴ (ἐπιστήμη), although he several times mentions τὰ ἠθικὰ and ἠθικοὶ λόγοι.) Ethical science is for the individual what political science is for the community (i. 2).

In every variety of human action, in each separate art and science, the agents, individual or collective, propose to themselves the attainment of some *good* as the end and object of their proceedings. Ends are multifarious, and good things are multifarious: but good, under one shape or another, is always the thing desired by every one, and the determining cause of human action (οὗ πάντα ἐφίεται)—i. 1.

Sometimes the action itself, or the exercise of the powers implied in the action, is the end sought, without anything beyond. Sometimes there is an ulterior end, or substantive business, to be accomplished by means of the action and lying beyond it. In this latter class of cases, the ulterior end is the real good : better than the course of action used to accomplish it—" the external results are naturally (πέφυκε) better than the course of action " (i. 1). Taking this as a general position, it is subject to many exceptions : but the word πέφυκε seems to signify only that such is naturally and ordinarily the case, not that the reverse never occurs.

Again some ends are comprehensive and supreme ; others, partial and subordinate. The subordinate ends are considered with reference to the supreme, and pursued as means to their accomplishment. Thus the end of the bridle-maker is subservient to that of the horseman, and the various operations of war to the general scheme of the commander. The supreme, or *architectonic*, ends, are superior in eligibility to the subordinate, or *ministerial*, which, indeed, are pursued only for the sake of the former.

One end (or one *good*), as subordinate, is thus included in another end (or another good) as supreme. The same end may be supreme with regard to one end different from itself, and subordinate with regard to another. The end of the general is supreme with reference to that of the soldier or the maker of arms, subordinate with reference to that of the statesman. In this scale of comprehensiveness of ends there is no definite limit : we may suppose ends more and more comprehensive as we please, and we come from thence to form the idea of one most comprehensive and sovereign end, which includes under it every other without exception—with reference to which all other ends stand in the relation either of parts or of means—and which is itself never in any case pursued for the sake of any other or independent end. The end thus conceived is the *Sovereign Good of man*, or *The Good—The Summum Bonum*—Τἀγαθὸν —Τὸ ἄριστον—Τἀνθρώπινον ἀγαθόν (i. 2).

To comprehend, to define, and to prescribe means for realizing the Sovereign Good, is the object of *Political Science*, the paramount and most architectonic Science of all, with regard to which all other Sciences are simply ministerial. It is the business of the political ruler to regulate the application of all other Sciences with reference to the production of this his End—to determine how far each shall be learnt and in what manner each shall be brought into practice—to enforce or forbid any system of human action according as it tends to promote the accomplishment of his supreme purpose—the Sovereign Good of the Community. Strategical, rhetorical, economical, science, are all to be applied so far as they conduce to this purpose and no farther : they are all simply ministerial; political science is supreme and self-determining (i. 2).

What *Political Science* is for the community, *Ethical*

Science is for the individual citizen. By this it is not meant that the individual is to be abstracted from society or considered as living apart from society : but simply that human action and human feeling is to be looked at from the point of view of the individual, mainly and primarily—and from the point of view of the society, only in a secondary manner : while in political science, the reverse is the case—our point of view is, first as regards the society ;—next, and subordinate to that, as regards the individual citizen (*See* Eth. Nic. vii. 8).

The object of the Ethical Science is, the Supreme Good of the individual citizen—the End of all Ends, with reference to his desires, his actions, and his feelings—the end which he seeks for itself and without any ulterior aim—the end which comprehends all his other ends as merely partial or instrumental and determines their comparative value in his estimation (i. 2, i. 4).

It is evident that this conception of an End of all Ends is what Kant would call an *Idea*—nothing precisely conformable to it, in its full extent, can ever exist in reality. No individual has ever been found, or ever will be found, with a mind so trained as to make every separate and particular desire subservient to some general preconceived End however comprehensive. But it is equally certain that this subordination of Ends one to another is a process performed to a greater or less degree in every one's mind, even in that of the rudest savage. No man can blindly and undistinguishingly follow every immediate impulse: the impulse, whatever it be, when it arises, must be considered more or less as it bears upon other pursuits and other objects of desire. This is an indispensable condition even of the most imperfect form of social existence. In civilized society, we find the process carried very far indeed in the minds of the greater number of individuals. Every man has in his view certain leading Ends, such as the maintenance of his proper position in society, the acquisition of professional success, the making of his fortune, the prosecution of his studies, &c., each of which is essentially paramount and architectonic, and with reference to which a thousand other ends are simply subordinate and ministerial. Suppose this process to be pushed farther, and you arrive at the idea of an End still more comprehensive, embracing every other end which the individual can aspire to, and forming the central point of an all-comprehensive scheme of life. Such a maximum, never actually attainable, but constantly approachable, in reality, forms the Object of Ethical Science. *Quorsum victuri gignimur?*

What is the Supreme Good—the End of all Ends? How are we to determine wherein it consists, or by what means it is to be attained—at least, as nearly

attained as the limitations of human condition per-
mit? Ethical Science professes to point out what
the end ought to be—Ethical precepts are suggestions for making the closest approaches to it which
are practicable. Even to understand what the end
is, is a considerable acquisition : since we thus know
the precise point to aim at, even if we cannot hit it
(i. 2).

The approaches which different men make towards forming this idea, of an End of Ends or of a
Supreme Good, differ most essentially : although there
seems a verbal agreement between them. Every
man speaks of *Happiness* as his End of Ends (ὀνόματι
ὁμολογεῖται, i. 4) : he wishes to live well or to do
well, which he considers to be the same as being
happy. But men disagree exceedingly in their
opinions as to that which constitutes happiness : nay
the same man sometimes places it in one thing,
sometimes in another—in health or in riches, according as he happens to be sick or poor.

There are however three grand divisions, in one
or other of which the opinions of the great majority
of mankind may be distributed. Some think that
happiness consists in a life of bodily pleasure (βίος
ἀπολαυστικός) : others, in a life of successful political
action or ambition (βίος πολιτικός) : others again,
in a life of speculative study and the acquisition of
knowledge (βίος θεωρητικός). He will not consent

to number the life of the (χρηματιστὴς) money-maker among them because he attains his end at the expense of other people and by a force upon their inclinations (this at least seems the sense of the words—ὁ γὰρ χρηματιστὴς βίαιός τίς ἐστι), and because wealth can never be *the good*, seeing that it is merely useful for the sake of ulterior objects.

(The reason which Aristotle gives for discarding from his catalogue the life of the *money-seeker*, while he admits that of the *pleasure-seeker* and the *honour-seeker*, appears a very inconclusive one. He believed them to be all equally mistaken in reference to real happiness : the two last just as much as the first : and certainly, if we look to prevalence in the world and number of adherents, the creed of the first is at least equal to that of the two last.)

The first of the three is the opinion of the mass, countenanced by many Sovereigns such as Sardanapalus—it is more suitable to animals than to men, in the judgment of Aristotle (i. 5).

Honour and glory—the reward of political ambition, cannot be the sovereign good, because it is a possession which the person honoured can never be sure of retaining : for it depends more upon the persons by whom he is honoured than upon himself, while the ideas which we form of the sovereign good suppose it to be something intimately belonging to us and hard to be withdrawn (i. 5). Moreover

those who aspire to honour, desire it not so much on
its own account as in order that they may have
confidence in their own virtue : so that it seems even
in their estimation as if virtue were the higher aim
of the two. But even virtue itself (meaning thereby
the simple possession of virtue as distinguished from
the active habitual exercise of it) cannot be the
sovereign good : for the virtuous man may pass his
life in sleep or in inaction—or he may encounter
intolerable suffering and calamity (i. 5).

Besides, Happiness as we conceive it, is an End
perfect, final, comprehensive and all-sufficient—an
end which we always seek on its own account and
never with a view to anything ulterior. But neither
honour, nor pleasure, nor intelligence, nor virtue,
deserves these epithets : each is an end special,
insufficient, and not final—for each is sought partly
indeed on its own account, but partly also on account
of its tendency to promote what we suppose to be
our happiness (i. 7). The latter is the only end
always sought exclusively for itself : including as it
always does and must do, the happiness of a man's
relatives, his children and his countrymen, or of all
with whom he has sympathies ; so that if attained,
it would render his life desirable and wanting for
nothing—ὃ μονούμενον, αἱρετὸν ποιεῖ τὸν βίον, καὶ
μηδενὸς ἐνδεᾶ (i. 7).

The remark which Aristotle here makes in respect

to the final aim or happiness of an individual—viz., that it includes the happiness of his family and his countrymen and of those with whom he has sympathies—deserves careful attention. It shews at once the largeness and the benevolence of his conceptions. We arrive thus at the same end as that proposed by political science—the happiness of the community: but we reach it by a different road, starting from the point of view of the individual citizen.

Having shewn that this Happiness, which is " our being's end and aim," does not consist in any special acquisition such as pleasure, or glory, or intelligence, or virtue, Aristotle adopts a different method to shew wherein it does consist. Every artist and every professional man (he says—i. 7), the painter, the musician, &c., has his peculiar business to do, and the *Good* of each artist consists in doing his business well and appropriately. Each separate portion of man, the eye, the hand and the foot, has its peculiar function: and in analogy with both these, man as such has his business and function, in the complete performance of which human Good consists. What is the business and peculiar function of Man, as Man? Not simply Life, for that he has in common with the entire vegetable and animal world: nor a mere sensitive Life, for that he has in common with all Animals: it must be something which he has, apart both from plants and animals—viz., an active life in conformity with reason (πρακτική τις τοῦ λόγου ἔχοντος); or the exercise of Reason as a directing and superintending force, and the exercise of the appetites, passions, and capacities, in a manner conformable to Reason. This is the special and peculiar business of man : it is what every man performs either well or ill : and the *virtue* of a man is that whereby he is enabled to perform it well. The Supreme Good of humanity, therefore, consisting as it does in the due performance of this special business of man, is to be found in the virtuous activity of our rational and appetitive soul : assuming always a life of the ordinary length, without which no degree of mental perfection would suffice to attain the object. The full position will then stand thus—" Happiness, or the highest good of a human being, consists in the working of the soul and in a course of action, pursuant to reason and conformable to virtue, throughout the full continuance of life."

(The argument respecting a man's proper business (ἔργον) and virtue (ἀρετή) seems to be borrowed from Plato—Republic, i. c. 23, p. 352 ; c. 24, p. 353. Compare also Xenophon—Memorabilia, iv. 2. 14.)

This explanation is delivered by Aristotle as a mere outline, which he seems to think that any one may easily fill up (i. 7). And he warns us not to require a greater degree of precision than the subject admits of : since we ought to be content with a rough approximation to the truth, and with conclusions which are not universally true, but only true in the majority of instances, such being the nature of the premises with which we deal (i. 3).

Having determined in this manner what Happiness or the Supreme Good consists in, Aristotle next shews that the explanation which he gives of it conforms in a great degree to the opinions previously delivered by eminent philosophers, and fulfils at least all the requisite conditions which have ever been supposed to belong to Happiness (i. 8). All philosophers have from very early times agreed in distributing good things into three classes — *Mental*, *Corporeal*, and *External*. Now the first of these classes is incomparably the highest and most essentially *good* of the three : and the explanation which Aristotle gives of happiness ranks it in the first class.

Again, various definitions of happiness have been delivered by eminent authorities more or less ancient (πολλοὶ καὶ παλαιοί). Eudoxus laid down the principle that happiness consists in pleasure : others have maintained the opinion that it is entirely independent both of pleasure and pain—that the former is no good, and the latter no evil (i. 12, vii. 11–13, x. 1. 2). Some have placed happiness in virtue : others in prudence : others in a certain sort of wisdom (σοφία

τις) : others have added to the definition this condition, that pleasure or external prosperity should be
coupled with the above-mentioned objects (i. 8).
The moral doctrines propounded by Zeno and Epicurus were therefore in no way new : how far the
reasonings by which these philosophers sustained
them were new we cannot judge accurately, from the
loss of the treatises of Eudoxus and others to which
Aristotle makes reference.

Now, in so far as virtue is introduced, the explanation of Happiness given by Aristotle coincides with
these philosophers and improves upon them by sub-
stituting the active exercise of virtuous habits in
place of the mere possession of virtue. And in
regard to pleasure, the man who has once acquired
habits of virtuous agency stands in no need of pleasure from without, as a foreign accessory : for he finds
pleasure in his own behaviour, and he would not be
denominated virtuous unless he did so : " Now (he
says) their life stands in no need of pleasure, like an
extraneous appendage, but has pleasure in itself "
(ii. 8). Again, ii. 3, he says that " the symptom of a
perfect habit is the pleasure or pain which ensues
upon the performance of the acts in which the habit
consists : for the man who abstains from bodily pleasures and rejoices in doing so, is temperate, while he
who does it reluctantly and painfully, is intemperate.
And the man who sustains dangers with pleasure, or

at least without pain, is courageous : if with pain, he is a coward.   For ethical virtue has reference to our pleasures and pains : it is on account of pleasure that we commit vicious acts, and on account of pain that we shrink from virtuous performances.   Wherefore, as Plato directs, we ought to be trained at once from our infancy by some means or other so as to feel pleasure and pain from the proper sources : for that is the right education."

Moreover, the man who is in the active exercise of virtue derives his pleasure from the performance of that which is the appropriate business of humanity, so that all his pleasures are *conformable to the pleasures natural to man* and therefore consistent with each other : whereas the pleasures of most people are contradictory and inconsistent with each other, because they are not conformable to our nature (i. 8).

It is not easy to understand perfectly what Aristotle means by saying that the things agreeable to the majority of mankind are not things agreeable by nature.   The construction above put upon this expression seems the only plausible one—that those pleasures which inhere in the performance of the appropriate business of man, are to be considered as our natural pleasures; those which do not so inhere, as not natural pleasures : inasmuch as they arise out of circumstances foreign to the performance of our appropriate business.

This however hardly consists with the explanation which Aristotle gives of τὸ φύσει—in another place and with reference to another subject. In the Magna Moralia (i. 34, pp. 1194–1195 Bek.), in distinguishing between *natural* justice (τὸ δίκαιον φύσει) and *conventional* justice (τὸ δίκαιον νόμῳ), he tells us that *the naturally just* is that which most commonly remains just. (Similarly Ethic. Eudem. iv. 14, p. 1217 Bek.) That which exists by nature (he says) may be changed by art and practice; the left hand may by these means be rendered as strong as the right in particular cases, but if in the greater number of cases and for the longer portion of time the left remains left and the right remains right, this is to be considered as existing by nature.

If we are to consider that arrangement as *natural* which we find to prevail in the greatest number of cases and for the greatest length of time, then undoubtedly the pleasures arising out of virtuous active behaviour must be regarded as less natural than those other pleasures which Aristotle admits to form the enjoyment of the majority of mankind.

But again there is a third passage, respecting nature and natural arrangements, which appears scarcely reconcilable with either of the two opinions just noticed. In Eth. Nicom. ii. 1 : " Ethical virtue is a result of habit, whence it is evident that not one of the ethical virtues exists in us by nature. For none of those things which exist by nature is altered by habit. For example, the stone which naturally moves downwards cannot be habituated to move upwards, not even if a man should endeavour so to habituate it by throwing it upwards ten thousand times; nor in like manner fire downwards: nor can any other of the things formed by nature in one way be changed by habit to any other than that natural way. Virtues therefore are not generated in us either *by* nature, or *contrary* to nature; but we are formed by nature so as to be capable of receiving them, and we are perfected in them through the influence of habit."

If it be true that nothing which exists in one manner by nature can be changed by habit so as to exist in another manner, I do not see how the assertion contained in the passage above cited out of the Magna Moralia can be reconciled with it, where we are told—" For even things which exist *by nature partake of change.* Thus if we all should practise throwing with the left hand, we should become ambidextrous: but still it is the left hand by nature, and the right hand is not the less better by nature than the left, although we should do everything with the left as we do with the right." (Mag. Mor. i. 34, *ut sup.*) In the one case he illustrates the meaning of natural properties by the comparative aptitudes of the right and left hand: in the other by the downward tendency of the stone. The idea is plainly different in the one case and in the other.

On the other hand, there seems to be not less variance between the one passage quoted out of the Nicomacheian Ethics and the other. For in the passage last quoted, we are told that none of the ethical virtues is generated in us by nature—neither by nature, nor contrary to nature: nature makes us fit to receive them, habit introduces and creates them—an observation perfectly true and accurate. But if this was the sentiment of Aristotle, how could he also believe that the pleasures arising out of the active manifestation of ethical virtue were the natural pleasures of man? If ethical virtue does not come by nature, the pleasures belonging to it cannot come by nature either.

On the whole, these three passages present a variance which I am unable to reconcile in the meaning which Aristotle annexes to the very equivocal word—*nature.*

Although Aristotle tells us that the active exercise of the functions of the soul according to virtue confers happiness, yet he admits that a certain measure of external comfort and advantages must be superadded as an indispensable auxiliary and instrument. Disgusting ugliness, bad health, low birth, loss of friends and relatives or vicious conduct of friends and relatives, together with many other misfortunes, are sufficient to sully the blessed condition of the most virtuous man (ῥυπαίνουσι τὸ μακάριον—i. 8)— for which reason it is that some persons have ranked both virtue and good fortune as co-ordinate ingredients equally essential to happiness : and have doubted also whether it can ever be acquired either by teaching, or by training, or by any other method except chance or Divine inspiration. To suppose that so magnificent a boon is conferred by chance, would be an absurdity : it is a boon not unworthy indeed of the Divine nature to confer; but still the magnificence of it will appear equally great and equally undeniable, if we suppose it to be acquired by teaching or training. And this is really the proper account to give of the way in which Happiness is acquired : for the grand and primary element in it, is the virtuous agency of the soul, which is undoubtedly acquired by training : while external advantages, though indispensable up to a certain limit, are acquired only as secondary helps and instruments. The creation of these virtuous habits among the citizens is one of the chief objects of political science and legislation : when once acquired, they are the most lasting and ineffaceable of all human possessions : and as they are created by special training, they may be imparted to every man not disqualified by some natural defect of organization, and may thus be widely diffused throughout the community (i. 9).

This is an important property. If happiness be supposed to be derived from the possession of wealth or honour or power, it can only be possessed by a small number of persons. For these three considered as objects of human desire, are essentially comparative. A man does not think himself rich, or honoured, or powerful, unless he becomes so to a degree above the multitude of his companions and neighbours.

Aristotle insists most earnestly that the only way of acquiring the character proper for happiness is by a course of early and incessant training in virtuous action. Moral teaching, he says, will do little or nothing, unless it be preceded by, or at least coupled with, moral training. Motives must be applied sufficient to ensure performance of what is virtuous and abstinence from what is vicious, until such a course of conduct becomes habitual, and until a disposition is created to persevere in them. It is the business of the politician and the legislator to employ their means of working upon the citizens for the purpose of enforcing this training. It is not with virtue (he says) as it is with those faculties which we receive ready-made from nature, as for example, the external senses. We do not acquire the faculty of sight by often seeing, but we have it from nature and then exercise it: whereas with regard to virtue, we obtain our virtues by means of a previous course of virtuous action, just as we learn other arts. For those things which we must learn in order to do, we learn by actually doing: thus by building we become builders, and by harping we become harpers: by doing just and temperate and courageous actions, we become just and temperate and courageous. All legislators try, some in a better and others in a worse manner, to *ethise* (ἐθίζοντες)—to create habits among—the citizens for the purpose of making them good. "In one word habits are created by repeated action, wherefore our actions must be determined in a suitable way, for according as they differ, so will our habits differ. Nor is the difference small whether we are *ethised* in one way or in another, from our youth upwards: the difference is very great, or rather it *is everything*" (ii. 1).

Neither an ox, nor a horse, can acquire such habits, and therefore neither of them can be called happy: even a child cannot be called so, except from the hope and anticipation of what he will become in future years.

It may appear somewhat singular that Aristotle characterises a child as incapable of happiness, since in common language a child when healthy and well treated is described as peculiarly happy. But happiness, as Aristotle understands it, is something measured more by the estimate of the judicious spectator than by the sentiment of the man in whose bosom it resides. No person is entitled to be called

happy, whom the intelligent and reflective observer
does not *macarise* (or *endæmonise*), or whose condition he would not desire more or less to make his
own.   Now the life of a child, even though replete
with all the enjoyments belonging to childhood, is
not such as any person in the state of mind of a
mature citizen could bring himself to accept (i. 10,
x. 3).   The test to which Aristotle appeals, either
tacitly or openly, seems always to be the judgment
of the serious man (i. 8, x. 5).   It is no sufficient
proof of happiness that the person who feels it is
completely satisfied with his condition and does not
desire anything beyond.   Such self-satisfaction is
indeed necessary, but is not by itself sufficient: it
must be farther confirmed by the judgment of
persons without—not of the multitude, who are apt
to judge by a wrong standard—nor of princes, who
are equally incompetent, *and who have never tasted
the relish of pure and liberal pleasures* (x. 6)—but of
the virtuous and worthy, who have arrived at the
most perfect condition attainable by human beings
(x. 5, x. 6, x. 8).

The different standard adopted by the many and
by the more discerning few, in estimating human
happiness, is again touched upon in Politica, vii. 1
It is in some respects treated more clearly and
simply in this passage than in the Ethics.   Both the
Many and the Few (he says) agree that in order to

constitute Happiness, there must be a coincidence of the three distinct kinds of Good things—The Mental —The Corporeal—The External. But with respect to the proportions in which the three ought to be intermingled, a difference of opinion arises. Most persons are satisfied with a very moderate portion of mental excellence, while they are immoderate in their desire for wealth and power (" For of virtue they think that they have a sufficiency, whatever be the quantity they have ; but of wealth and possessions they seek the excess without bound."—Pol. vii. 1). On the other hand, the opinion sanctioned by the few of a higher order of mind, and adopted by Aristotle, was, that Happiness was possessed in a higher degree by those who were richly set forth with moral and intellectual excellence and only moderately provided with external advantages, than by those in regard to whom the proportion was reversed (*ib.*). The same difference of estimate, between the few and the many, is touched upon Polit. vii. 13, where he says that men in general esteem external advantages to be the causes of happiness : which is just as if they were to say that the cause why a musician played well was his lyre, and not his proficiency in the art.

In this chapter of the Politica (vii. 13), he refers to the Ethica in a singular manner. Having stated that the point of first importance is, to deter-

mine wherein happiness consists, he proceeds to say
—" We have said also in the Ethics, *if there be any
good in that treatise* (εἴ τι τῶν λόγων ἐκείνων ὄφελος),
that it (happiness) is the active exertion and perfected habit of virtue."—This is a singular expression—" if there be any good in the Ethics "—it
seems rather to fall in with the several passages in
that treatise in which he insists upon the inherent
confusion and darkness of the subject-matter.

The definition of what happiness really is seems to
be one of the weak points of Aristotle's treatise.   In
a work addressed to the public, it is impossible to
avoid making the public judges of the pleasure and
pain, the happiness and unhappiness of individuals.
A certain measure of self-esteem on the part of the
individual, and a certain measure of esteem towards
him on the part of persons without, come thus to be
regarded as absolutely essential to existence.   Without these, life would appear intolerable to any spectator without, though the individual himself might
be degraded enough to cling to it.   But these are
secured by the ordinary morality of the age and of
the locality.   The question arises as to degrees of
virtue beyond the ordinary level : Are we sure that
such higher excellence contributes to the happiness
of the individual who possesses it ?   Assuming that
it does so contribute, are we certain that the acces-
sion of happiness which he thereby acquires is

greater than he would have acquired by an increase of his wealth and power, his virtue remaining still at the ordinary level? These are points which Aristotle does not establish satisfactorily, although he professes to have done so: nor do I think that they are capable of being established. The only ground on which a moralist can inculcate aspirations after the higher degrees of virtue, is, the gain which thereby accrues to the happiness of others, not to that of the individual himself.

Aristotle appeals to God as a proof of the superiority of an internal source of happiness to an external source—vii. 1, "using God as a witness who is happy and blessed, yet not through any external good, but through Himself and from His own nature." Again, vii. 3, "For at leisure God would be happy, and the whole universe (κόσμος), who have no external actions except such as are proper to themselves"—in proof of the superiority of a life of study and speculation to a life of ambition and political activity. The same argument is insisted upon in Eth. Nic. x. 8. It is to be observed that the Κόσμος as well as God is here cited as experiencing happiness.

The analogy to which Aristotle appeals here is undoubtedly to a certain extent a just one. The most perfect happiness which we can conceive—our Idea, to use Kant's phrase, of perfect happiness—is that of a being who is happy in and for his own nature, with the least possible aid from external circumstances—a being whose nature or habits dispose him only to acts, the simple performance of which confers happiness. But is this true of the perfectly virtuous nature and habits? Does the simple performance of the acts to which they dispose us, always confer happiness? Is not the existence of a very high standard of virtuous exigency in a man's mind, a constant source of self-dissatisfaction, from the difficulty of acting up to his own ideas of what is becoming and commendable?

That the most virtuous nature is in itself and essentially the most happy nature, is a point highly questionable—to say the least of it : and even if we admit the fact, we must at the same time add that it cannot appear to be so to ordinary persons without. The internal pleasures of a highly virtuous man cannot be properly appreciated by any person not of similar character. So that unless a person be himself disposed to believe it, you could find no means of proving it to him. To a man not already virtuous, you cannot bring this argument persuasively home for the purpose of inducing him to become so.

In regard to prudence and temperance, indeed, qualities in the first instance beneficial to himself, it is clear that the more perfectly he possesses them, the greater and more assured will be his happiness.

But in regard to virtuous qualities, beneficial in the first instance to others and not to himself, it can by no means be asserted that the person who possesses these qualities in the highest degree is happier than one who possesses them in a more moderate and ordinary degree.

Aristotle indeed says that *the being just* necessarily includes the having pleasure in such behaviour : for we do not call a man just or liberal unless he has a pleasure in justice or liberality (Eth. Nic. i. 8). But this does not refute the supposition, that another man, less just or liberal than he, may enjoy *greater happiness* arising out of other tastes and other conduct.

In order to sustain the conclusion of Aristotle respecting the superior happiness of the virtuous man, it is necessary to assume that the pleasures of self-esteem and self-admiration are generically distinguished from other pleasures and entitled to a preference in the eyes of every right judging person. And Aristotle does seem to assume something of this nature. He says—x. 3—" Or that pleasures differ in kind ? For the pleasures arising from the honourable are different from those arising from the base ; and it is not the case that the unjust man experiences the pleasure of the just, or he that is unmusical that of the musician." The inherent difference between various pleasures is again touched

upon x. 5—"And since the functions differ in
goodness and badness—some of them being objects of
desire, others of them to be eschewed, and others of
them neither—so is it likewise with the pleasures :
for each function has its own pleasures. The pleasure then that is proper to the function of good is
good, and that which is proper to the function of
bad is bad; for the desires of things honourable are
praiseworthy, those of things base are to be blamed.
And the pleasures attaching to them are more
proper to the functions than are the appetencies
themselves." In the next chapter, in that remarkable passage where he touches upon the predilec-
tions of men in power for the society of jesters and
amusing companions (" The many have recourse to
the amusements of those that are accounted happy ")
—" For it is not in kingly power that you find
either virtue or intellect, on which the higher functions of man depend. Nay, not if princes *who have
never tasted the relish of pure and liberal pleasure*,
have recourse to the pleasures of the body, on which
account these must be thought the more desirable.
For children consider those things to be best that
are held in honour among themselves."

Here we have a marked distinction drawn between
the different classes of pleasures—some being cha-
racterised as good, some bad, some indifferent. The
best of all are those which the virtuous man enjoys,

and which *he* considers the best: the pleasures inseparably annexed to virtuous agency. These pleasures
are thus assumed to be of a purer and more exalted
character, and to deserve a decided preference over
every other class of pleasures. And if this be
assumed, the superior happiness of the virtuous man
follows as a matter of course.

I should observe that Aristotle considers happiness
to consist in the exercise of the faculties agreeably to
virtue (ἐνέργεια κατ᾿ ἀρετὴν)—the *pleasure* (ἡδονὴ)
is something different from the exercise (ἐνέργεια)—
inseparably attending it, indeed, yet not the same—
"conjoined with the functions (ἐνεργείαις), and the
two are so inseparable as to raise a question whether
the function is not identical with the pleasure"
(x. 5). And he says, x. 7—"We think that pleasure
should be mixed up (παραμεμίχθαι) with happiness."

It seems to be in the sense of self-esteem, which
constitutes the distinctive mark of virtuous agency,
that Aristotle supposes happiness to consist: the
pleasure he supposes to be an inseparable concomitant, but yet not the same. The self-esteem is doubtless often felt in cases where a man is performing a
painful duty—where the sum total of feelings accompanying the performance of the act is the very
reverse of pleasurable. But still the self-esteem, or
testimony of an approving conscience, is *per se* always
pleasurable, and is in fact the essential pleasure

inherent in vir_ious behaviour. I do not see the propriety of the distinction here taken by Aristotle. He puts it somewhat differently, Polit. vii. 1— " Living happily consists either in joy or in virtue to men, or in both." And Polit. viii. 5—" For happiness is a compound of both these (honour and pleasure)." So Polit. viii. 3.

Happiness (again he says—Polit. vii. 13, p. 440 E. p. 286) consists in the perfect employment and active exercise of virtue : and that *absolutely* (or under the most favourable external conditions) — not under limitation (ἐξ ὑποθέσεως) or subject to very trying and difficult circumstances. For a man of virtue may be so uncomfortably placed that he has no course open to him except a choice of evils, and can do nothing but make the best of a bad position. Such a man will conduct himself under the pressure of want or misfortune as well as his case admits : but happiness is out of his reach. (Compare Eth. Nic. i. 10.) To be happy, it is necessary that he should be so placed as to be capable of aspiring to the accomplishment of positive good and advantage—he must be admitted to contend for the great prizes, and to undertake actions which lead to new honours and to benefits previously unenjoyed : he must be relieved from the necessity of struggling against overwhelming calamities.

Aristotle tells us in the beginning of the Ethics

(Eth. Nic. i. 3)—" But there is so much difference of opinion and so much error respecting what is honourable and just, of which political science treats, that these properties of human action seem to exist merely by positive legal appointment, and not by nature.   And there is the same sort of error respecting what things are good."   If there be this widespread error and dissension among mankind with respect to the determining of what is good and just, what standard has Aristotle established for the purpose of correcting it?   I do not find that he has established any standard, nor even that he has thought it necessary to make the attempt.   There are indeed a great number of observations, and many most admirable observations in his Treatise, on the various branches of Virtue and Vice : many which tend to conduct the mind of the reader unconsciously to the proper standard : but no distinct announcement of any general principle, whereby a dispute between two dissentient moralists may be settled.   When he places virtue in a certain mediocrity between excess on one side and defect on the other, this middle point is not in any way marked or discoverable : it is a point not fixed, but variable according to the position of the individual agent, and is to be determinable in every case by right reason and according to the judgment of the prudent man—" in the mean *with reference to ourselves*, as *it has been determined by reason*, and *as the prudent man* (ὁ φρόνιμος) *would determine it*" (Eth. Nic. ii. 6). But though the decision is thus vested in the prudent man, no mention is made of the principle which the appointed arbiter would follow in delivering his judgment, assuming a dispute to arise.

In a previous part of Chapter II., he defines " the mean with reference to ourselves" to be " that which neither exceeds, nor falls short of, *the rule of propriety* (τοῦ δέοντος). But this is not one, nor is it the same to all."

To render this definition sufficient and satisfactory, Aristotle ought to have pointed out to us how we are to find out that *rule of propriety* (τὸ δέον) which marks and constitutes the medium point, of actions and affections, *in relation to ourselves*—this medium point being in his opinion *virtue*. To explain what is meant by a medium *in relation to ourselves*, by the words τὸ δέον, *the rule of propriety*, is only a change of language, without any additional information.

Thus the capital problem of moral philosophy still remains unsolved.

It is remarkable that Aristotle in some parts of his treatise states very distinctly what this problem is, and what are the points essential to its solution: he speaks as if he were fully aware of that which was wanting to his own treatise, and as if he were preparing to supply the defect: but still the promise is

never realized. Take for example the beginning of
Book VI. Eth. Nic.

" Since it has been already laid down, that we
ought to choose the middle point and not either the
excess or the defect—and since the middle point is
that which right reason determines—let us distinguish what that is. For in all the mental habits
which have been described, as well as in all others
also, there is a certain aim, by a reference to which
the rational being is guided either in relaxing
or in restricting: and there is a certain definite
boundary of those medial points, which we affirm
to exist between excess and defect, determinable
according to right reason. To speak thus, however,
is indeed correct enough, but it gives no distinct
information (οὐθὲν δὲ σαφές): for in all other modes
of proceeding which are governed by scientific principles it is quite just to say that you ought neither
to work nor to rest more than is sufficient nor less
than is sufficient, but to a degree midway between
the two and agreeably to right reason. But a man
who has only this information would be no wiser
than he was before it, any more than he would know
what things he ought to apply to his body, by being
simply told that he must apply such things as medical science and as the medical practitioner directed.
Wherefore, with respect also to the habits of the soul
we must not be content with merely giving a general

yet the wise man might not recognise him as happy.
Or he might be in a state from which he was very
anxious to escape, and yet the wise man might
refuse to pronounce him unhappy. Seneca indeed
(Epist. IX.) seems to say the contrary of this, and
to cite both Epicurus and the Stoics as authorities—
" Non est beatus, esse se qui non putat "—and
then he eludes the difficulty by contending—" Nisi
sapienti sua non placent : omnis stultitia laborat fas-
tidio sui."

In appreciating the moral systems of the ancients,
however, it is of great moment to keep in view the
way in which they understood and defined *Happiness*.
The ethical ἀρχὴ from which they started was, the
injunction upon every individual to pursue his own
happiness. But this, if allowed to be interpreted by
the individual himself, would have led to endless
errors and deviations, according to every man's
different taste. Accordingly they laid down the
scheme of one particular state of mind and circumstances, as constituting the maximum of individual
happiness, or the only thing which they were willing
to call happiness. Each of the philosophical sects
did this, though all of them did not lay down the
same scheme. To pursue happiness, was to follow
the scheme of happiness prescribed by the wise man:
whoever did not follow this, whatever his own tastes
or inclinations might be, was not allowed to be

obeying the natural dictate of pursuing his own happiness.

It is easy to see that when the definition of happiness was so restricted as to embrace only that which the wise man would call happiness, the main observances of morality would be quite sure to be comprehended in it. The wise and virtuous man would not esteem any other man happy who was not wise and virtuous. He might perhaps not account another man happy with wisdom and virtue alone, though accompanied by great external disadvantages : but the presence of these lofty mental qualities he would deem absolutely indispensable.

The ancient moralists considered the happiness of the individual agent as the sole and exclusive end : but they also considered that virtuous conduct was the sole and exclusive means to that end. In this manner the interests and happiness of persons other than the individual came to be inseparably intermingled in their theories with the interests and happiness of the individual himself, although the latter alone formed the original point of departure.

In studying their moral treatises, this confusion will often be found both very prevalent and very perplexing. When they speak of *good*, it is sometimes *good* with reference to the interests and happiness of the individual agent—sometimes *good*, with reference to the interests and happiness of society.

must be known, before we can know what *living well* is.

I think that this σκόπος or end, which Aristotle alludes to in the beginning of the Sixth Book as not having been yet made clear, appears to be more distinctly brought out in a previous passage than it is in any portion of the Treatise after the beginning of the Sixth Book. In Book IV. 6, Aristotle treats of the virtues and defects connected with behaviour in social intercourse : the *obsequious* at one extreme, the *peevish* or *quarrelsome* at the other : and the becoming medium, though it had no special name, which lay between them. Speaking of the person who adopts this becoming medium, he says—" We have said generally, then, that he will associate with people as he ought; and having, moreover, a constant reference to what is honourable and what is expedient, he will aim at not giving pain or at contributing pleasure."

Again in regard to Temperance—iii. 11—he states the σκόπος of the temperate man—" What things have a reference to health or vigour, and are agreeable, these he desires in measure and as he ought; as well as the other agreeable things that are not opposed to these, either as being contrary to what is honourable or as being beyond his fortune. For he that desires things agreeable, which yet are contrary to what is honourable or beyond his fortune, loves these pleasures more than they are worth. But not so with the temperate man, who lives according to right reason."

These passages are not very distinct, as an explanation of the proper σκόπος: but I cannot find any passages after the beginning of the Sixth Book which are more distinct than they: or perhaps, equally distinct.

In one passage of the Seventh Book, Aristotle refers, though somewhat obscurely, to the average degree of virtue exhibited by the mass of mankind as the standard to be consulted when we pronounce upon excess or defect (vii. 7).

Aristotle seems in some passages to indicate pleasure and pain as the end with reference to which actions or dispositions are denominated *good* and *evil*. He says—vii. 11—" To theorise respecting pleasure and pain, is the business of the political philosopher: for he is the architect of that end with reference to which we call each matter either absolutely good or absolutely evil. Moreover, it is indispensable to institute an enquiry respecting them: for we have explained ethical virtue and vice as referring to pleasures and pains: and most people affirm happiness to be coupled with pleasure : for which reason they have named τὸ μακάριον ἀπὸ τοῦ χαίρειν."

In Book VIII. 9–10, the σκόπος is indeed stated very clearly, but *not as such*—not as if Aristotle

intended to make it serve as such, or thought that it
ought to form the basis upon which our estimate of
what is the proper middle point should be found. In
viii. 9–10, he tells us that all justice and benevolence
(τὸ δίκαιον καὶ ἡ φιλία) is a consequence and an
incident of established communion among human
beings (κοινωνία)—that the grand communion of
all, which comprehends all the rest, is the *Political
Communion*—that the end and object of the *Political
Communion*, as well that for which it was originally
created as that for which it subsists and continues, is
the common and lasting advantage (τὸ κοινῇ σύμφερον)
—that all other communions, of relations, friends,
fellow-soldiers, neighbours, &c., are portions of the
all-comprehensive political communion, and aim at
realizing some partial advantage to the constituent
members. These chapters are very clear and very
important, and they announce plainly enough *the
common and lasting interest* as the foundation and
measure of justice as well as of benevolence. But
they do not apply the same measure, to the qualities
which had been enumerated in the Books prior to
the Sixth, as a means of ascertaining where the
middle point is to be found which is alleged to constitute virtue. Nevertheless, Aristotle tells us that it
is in the highest degree difficult to find the middle
point which constitutes virtue (ii. 9).

It might seem at first sight not easy for Aristotle,

consistently with the plan of his treatise, to point out any such standard or measure.   For none can be mentioned, with any tolerable pretensions to admissibility, except that of *tendency to promote happiness*— the happiness both of the individual agent and of the society to which he belongs.   But as he had begun by introducing the ideas of reason and virtue as media for explaining what happiness was, there would have been at least an apparent incongruity in reverting back to the latter as a means of clearing up what was obscure in the former.   I say—*at least an apparent incongruity*—because after all the incongruity is more apparent than real.   If we carefully preserve the distinction between the happiness of the individual agent and the happiness of the Society to which he belongs, it will appear that Aristotle might without any inconsistency have specified the latter as being the object to which reason has regard, in regulating and controlling the various affections of each individual.

Wherein consists the happiness of an individual man?   In a course of active exertion of the soul conformably to virtue : *virtue* being understood to consist in a certain mediocrity of our various affections as determined by *right reason*.

When we next enquire, to what standard does *right reason* look in making this determination ? it may without inconsistency be answered — *Right*

reason determines the proper point of mediocrity by
a reference to *happiness generally*—that is, to the
happiness of society at large, including that of the
individual agent in question—in other words, to *the
common and lasting advantage*, which Aristotle de-
scribes as the grand object of the statesman.   There
is no inconsistency in reverting to happiness, thus
explained, as the standard by which right reason
judges in controlling our different affections.

In all moral enquiries, it is of the greatest importance to keep in view the happiness of the
individual, and the happiness of the society at large,
as two distinct and separate objects—which coincide
indeed ὡς ἐπὶ τὸ πολύ, in the majority of instances
and with regard to the majority of individuals—but
which do not coincide necessarily and universally,
nor with regard to every individual.   A particular
man may be placed in such a position, or animated
with such feelings, that his happiness may be pro-
moted by doing what is contrary to the happiness of
the society.   He will under these circumstances do
what is *good* for himself but *bad* for others: he will
do what is morally wrong, and will incur the blame
of society.   In speaking of *good* and *evil* it is always
necessary to keep in mind, that what is *good* for an
individual may be *bad* for the society: I mean,
understanding the words *good for an individual* in
the most comprehensive sense, as including all that

he has to suffer from the unfavourable sentiments of society. Much confusion has arisen from moralists speaking of good and evil absolutely, without specifying whether they meant *good* for the individual or for the society : more particularly in the writings of the ancient philosophers.

From the manner in which Aristotle arrives at his definition of what constitutes happiness, we might almost suppose that he would have been led to the indication of the happiness of society at large as the standard for right reason to appeal to. For in examining what is the proper business of man in general, he has recourse to the analogy of the various particular arts and professions—the piper, the statuary, the carpenter, the carrier, &c. Each has his particular business and walk of action, and in the performance of that business consists *the good and the well* in his case (i. 7). So in like manner there is a special business for man in general, in the performance of which we are to seek human good.

Now this analogy of particular artists and professional men might have conducted Aristotle to the idea of the general happiness of society as a standard. For the business of every artist or artisan consists in conducing to the comfort, the protection, or the gratification of the public, each in his particular walk : professional excellence for them consists in accomplishing this object perfectly. For every special profession therefore the happiness of society at large, under one form or another, is introduced as the standard by which good and excellence are to be measured.

Apply this analogy to man in general, taken apart from any particular craft or profession. If each man, considered simply as such, has his appropriate business, in the good performance of which happiness for him consists, the standard of excellence in respect to such performance is to be found in its conduciveness to the happiness of society at large. It can be found nowhere else, if we are to judge according to the analogy of special arts and professions.

Until this want of a standard or measure is supplied, it is clear that the treatise of Aristotle is defective in a most essential point—a defect which is here admitted by himself in the first chapter of the Sixth Book. Nor is there any other way of supplying what is wanting except by reference to the general happiness of society, the end and object (as he himself tells us) of the statesman.

"What then," says Aristotle, "prevents our calling him happy who is in the active exercise of his soul agreeably to perfect virtue, and is sufficiently well furnished with external goods, not for a casual period but for a complete lifetime?" (i. 10). He thinks himself obliged to add, however, that this is not quite sufficient—for that after death a man will still be affected with sympathy for the good or bad fortunes and conduct of his surviving relatives, affected however faintly and slightly, so as not to deprive him of the title to be called *happy*, if on other grounds he deserves it. The deceased person sees the misfortunes of his surviving friends with something of the same kind of sympathetic interest, though less in degree, as is felt by a living person in following the representation of a tragedy (i. 11). The difference between a misfortune, happening during a man's life or after his death, is much greater than that between scenic representation of past calamities and actual reality (*ib.*).

It seems as if Aristotle was reluctantly obliged to make this admission—that deceased persons were at all concerned in the calamities of the living—more in deference to the opinions of others than in consequence of any conviction of his own. His language in the two chapters wherein he treats of it is more than usually hesitating and undecided: and in the beginning of Chapter XI., he says—" To have no interest whatever in the fortunes of their descendants and friends, seems exceedingly heartless and contrary to what we should expect'—he then, farther on, states it to be a great matter of doubt whether the dead experience either good or evil—but if anything of the kind does penetrate to them, it must be feeble and insignificant, so as to make no sensible difference to them.

II.

Aristotle distributes *good things* into three classes—the *admirable* or worshipful—the *praiseworthy*—the *potential.*

1. *Good*—as an End: that which is worthy of being honoured and venerated in itself and from its own nature, without regard to anything ulterior: that which comes up to our idea of perfection.

2. *Good*—as a means: that which is good, not on its own account nor in its own nature, but on account of certain ulterior consequences which flow from it.

3. *Good*—as a means, but not a certain and constant means: that which produces *generally*, but *not always*, ulterior consequences finally good: that which, in order to produce consequences in themselves good, requires to be coupled with certain concomitant conditions.

1. *Happiness* belongs to the first of these classes: it is put along with *the divine, the better, soul, intellect, the more ancient, the principle, the cause,* &c. (Mag. Moral. i. 2). Such objects as these, we contemplate with awe and reverence.

2. *Virtue* belongs to the second of the classes : it is good from the acts to which it gives birth, and from the end (happiness) which those acts, when sufficiently long continued, tend to produce.

3. *Wealth, power, beauty, strength, &c.* belong to the third class : these are generally *good* because under most circumstances they tend to produce happiness : but they may be quite otherwise, if a man's mind be so defectively trained as to dispose him to abuse them.

It is remarkable that this classification is not formally laid down and explained, but is assumed as already well known and familiar, in the Nicom. Ethics, i. 12 : whereas it is formally stated and explained in the Magna Moralia, i. 2.

Praise, according to Aristotle, " does not belong to the best things, but only to the second-best. The Gods are to be *macarised*, not *praised :*" the praise of the Gods must have reference to ourselves, and must be taken in comparison with ourselves and our acts and capacities : and this is ridiculously degrading, when we apply it to the majesty of the Gods. In like manner the most divine and perfect men deserve to be macarised rather than praised. " No man praises happiness, as he praises justice, but *macarises* (*blesses*) it as something more divine and better."

Happiness is to be numbered amongst the perfect

and worshipful objects—it is the ἀρχὴ for the sake
of which all of us do everything : and we consider
the principle and the cause of all good things to be
something divine and venerable (i. 12).

Since then Happiness is the action of the soul
conformably to perfect virtue, it is necessary to
examine what human virtue is : and this is the most
essential mark to which the true politician will direct
his attention (i. 13).

There are two parts of the soul—the rational and
the irrational. Whether these two are divisible in
fact, like the parts of the body, or whether they are
inseparable in fact, and merely susceptible of being
separately dealt with in reasoning, like the con-
cavity and convexity of a circle, is a matter not
necessary to be examined in the present treatise.
Aristotle speaks as if he considered this as really a
doubtful point.

Of the irrational soul, one branch is, the nutritive
and vegetative faculty, common to man with animals
and plants. The *virtue* of this faculty is not special
to man, but common to the vegetable and animal
world : it is in fact most energetic during sleep, at
the period when all virtue special to man is for the
time dormant (i. 13).

But the irrational soul has also another branch,
the appetites, desires, and passions : which are
quite distinct from reason, but may either resist

reason, or obey it, as the case may happen. It may thus in a certain sense be said to partake of reason, which the vegetative and nutritive faculty does not in any way. The virtue of this department of the soul consists in its due obedience to reason, as to the voice of a parent (i. 13).

Human virtue, then, distributes itself into two grand divisions—1. The virtue of the rational soul, or Intellectual Virtue. 2. The virtue of the semi-rational soul, or Ethical Virtue.

Perhaps the word *Excellence* more exactly corresponds to ἀρετὴ, than *Virtue*.

Intellectual excellence is both generated and augmented by teaching and experience. Ethical excellence by practical training. The excellence is not natural to us : but we are susceptible of being trained, and the training creates it. By training, according as it is either good or bad, all excellence is either created or destroyed: just as a man becomes a good or a bad musician, according as he has been subjected to a good or a bad mode of practice.

It is by doing the same thing many times that we acquire at last the habit of doing it—"For what things we have to learn to do, these we learn by doing " (ii. 1) : according as the things we are trained to do are good or bad, we acquire good habits or bad habits. By building we become builders, by playing on the harp we become harpers—good or indifferent,

according to the way in which we have practised.
All legislators wish and attempt to make their
citizens good, by means of certain habits: some
succeed in the attempt, others fail: and this is the
difference between a good and a bad government.
It is by being trained to do acts of justice and
courage that we become at last just and courageous
—" In one word, habits are generated by (a succes-
sion of) like operations: for this reason it is the
character of the operations performed which we
ought chiefly to attend to: for according to the
difference of these will be the habits which ensue.
It is therefore not a matter of slight difference
whether immediately from our earliest years we are
ethised in one way or in another—it makes a prodi-
gious difference—or rather, it makes the whole
difference" (ii. 1).

Uniform perseverance in action, then, creates a
habit: but of what nature is the required action to
be? In every department of our nature, where any
good result is to be produced, we may be disappointed of our result by two sorts of error: either
an excess or on the side of defect. To work or eat
too much, or too little, prevents the good effects of
training upon the health and strength: so with
regard to temperance, courage and the other virtues
—the man who is trained to fear everything and
the man who is trained to fear nothing, will alike

and temperate. If he does them, knowing what he does, intending what he does, and intending to do the acts for their own sake, then indeed he is just and temperate, but not otherwise. The productions of art carry their own merit along with them: a work of art is excellent or defective, whatever be the state of mind of the person who has executed it. But the acts of a man cannot be said to be justly or temperately done, unless there be a certain state of mind accompanying their performance by the doer: they may indeed be called just and temperate acts, meaning thereby that they are such as a just and temperate man would do, but the man who does them does not necessarily deserve these epithets. It is only by frequent doing of acts of this class that a man can acquire the habit of performing them intentionally and for themselves, in which consists the just and temperate character. To know what such acts are, is little or nothing: you must obey the precepts, just as you follow the prescriptions of a physician. Many men think erroneously that philosophy will teach them to be virtuous, without any course of action adopted by themselves (ii. 4).

Aristotle classifies the phenomena of the soul (the non-rational soul) into three—Passions—Capacities or Faculties—States. The first are the occasional affections—anger, fear, envy, joy, aversion—" in short, everything that is accompanied by pleasure or

pain" (ii. 5).   The second are, the capacities of being
moved by such affections—the affective faculties,
if one may so call them (*ib.*   So Eth. Eudem. ii. 2).
The third are, those habits according to which we are
said to be well or ill disposed towards this or that
particular affection : to be disposed to violent anger
or violent fear, is a bad habit.   Virtues and vices are
neither affections, nor faculties, but *habits*, either
good or bad.   This is the *genus* to which the virtues
belong (τῷ γένει—Eth. Nic. ii. 5).   Virtue is that
habit from the possession of which a man is called
good, and by which he performs well his appropriate
function (ii. 6).   It consists in a certain medium
between two extremes, the one of excess, the other
of defect—a medium not positive and absolute, but
variable and having reference to each particular
person and each particular case—neither exceeding
nor falling short of what is proper (ii. 6).   All ethical
virtue aims at the attainment of this middle point in
respect to our affections and actions—to exhibit each
on the proper occasions, in the proper degree, towards
the proper persons, &c.   This middle point is but
one, but errors on both sides of it are numberless : it
must be determined by reason and by the judgment
of the prudent man (ii. 6).

Virtue therefore, according to its essence and
generic definition (κατὰ μὲν τὴν οὐσίαν, καὶ τὸν λόγον
τὸν τί ἦν εἶναι λέγοντα), is a *certain mediocrity.*

But there are some actions and some affections which do not admit of mediocrity, and which imply at once in their names evil and culpability (ii. 6) —such as impudence, envy, theft, &c. Each of these names implies in its meaning a certain excess and defect, and does not admit of mediocrity: just as *temperance* and *courage* imply in their meaning the idea of mediocrity, and exclude both excess and defect.

Aristotle then proceeds to apply his general doctrine—that virtue or excellence consists in a medium between two extremes, both defects—to various different virtues. He again insists upon the extreme difficulty of determining where this requisite medium is, in each individual instance: either excess or defect is the easy and natural course. In finding and adhering to the middle point consists the *well*, the *rare*, the *praiseworthy*, the *honourable* (ii. 9). The extremes, though both wrong, are not always equally wrong: that which is the most wrong ought at any rate to be avoided: and we ought to be specially on our guard against the seductions of pleasure (*ib.*), since our natural inclinations carry us in that direction.

Aristotle so often speaks of the propriety of following *nature*, and produces *nature* so constantly as an authority and an arbiter, that it seems surprising to find him saying—"We must be on our guard answer as a matter of fact, but he will deny its force as a refutation. If it be not so (he will say) it ought to be so, and it will be so when men become improved. The like reply may be made with respect to ethical sanction, which, as men are now constituted, is certainly not directed exclusively towards the promotion of the social happiness. That this is true now, and always has been true, as a matter of fact is no ground of opposition to the philosopher who contends that it *ought* to be so.

Besides, it is admitted on all hands that the observance of ethical obligations is absolutely indispensable to ensure the safety and happiness of society; without such observance these ends could not possibly be attained. It may be said that these are not the *only* ends which ethical observances answer—it may further be said that they are ends attained not by any deliberate foregoing consciousness, but by hap-hazard. But still it is not the less true that the safety and happiness of society are the actual result of the establishment of ethical relations among its members, and that every adult person has a conviction that they are so.

Moreover, this grand end is common to all the separate exhibitions of ethical sentiment, in all times and places. The positive morality of one age agrees in this respect with the positive morality of another. But in respect to other accessory ends, not connected with the safety and happiness of society, the morality of one age differs very widely from that of another. There are endless divergences in matters of peculiar fancy and sentiment.

As positive morality has existed up to the present time, there are such accessory ends in every society, sometimes occupying as much attention as the main end. If we collect the list of all actions which are either approved or disapproved, esteemed or abhorred, it will not be found that *all* in the former list are actions which tend to the safety or happiness of the society—still less will it be found that all the latter list are actions which tend to the peril or misery or discomfort of the society. Such predicates will be true with regard to a certain number of the actions comprised in each list — but certainly not with regard to all.

That men have a tendency to love and esteem those beings who are causes of happiness to them, and to hate and dread those who occasion them suffering, is unquestionable. This is a tendency common to all mankind and observable in every different society. In so far as men feel and judge under the influence of this tendency, the positive morality of all societies is cast nearly upon the same mould, and assumes similar features.

But there are two points to be considered in addition to this general statement.

to be done *voluntarily*: if the agent shall be afterwards grieved and repentant for what he has done,
it is *involuntary*. If he be not repentant, though he
cannot be said to have done the deed *voluntarily*, yet
neither ought it to be called involuntary.

A distinction however is to be taken in regard to
ignorance, considered as a ground for calling the
action *involuntary*, and for excusing the agent. A
man drunk or in a violent passion, misbehaves
ignorantly, but not *through ignorance*: that is, ignorance is not the cause of his misbehaviour, but
drunkenness or rage. In like manner, every depraved person may be ignorant of his true interest,
or the rule which he ought to follow, but this sort of
ignorance does not render his behaviour *involuntary*,
nor entitle him to any indulgence. It must be ignorance with regard to some particular circumstance
connected with the special action which he is com-
mitting—ignorance of the person with whom, or the
instrument with which, or the subject matter in regard
to which he is dealing. Ignorance of this special
kind, if it be accompanied with subsequent sorrow
and repentance, constitutes an action involuntary,
and forms a reasonable ground for indulgence (ii. 1).

A *voluntary action*, then, is that of which the
beginning is in the agent—he knowing the particular circumstances under which he is acting. Some
persons have treated actions, performed through

passion or through desire, as *involuntary*: but this is an error. If this were true, neither children nor animals would be capable of voluntary action. Besides, it is proper, on some occasions, to follow the dictates both of anger and of desire : and we cannot be said to act involuntarily in these cases when we do exactly what we ought to do. Moreover sins from passions and sins from bad reasoning are alike voluntary or alike involuntary : both of them ought to be avoided : and the non-rational affections are just as much a part of human nature as reason is (ii. 1).

Having explained the proper meaning of voluntary and involuntary as applied to actions, Aristotle proceeds to define προαίρεσις (deliberate choice) ; which is most intimately connected with excellence, and which indeed affords a better test of disposition than actions themselves can do (ii. 2).

All premeditated choice is voluntary, but all voluntary action is not preconcerted. Children and animals are capable of voluntary action, but not of preconcerted action : sudden deeds, too, are voluntary, but not preconcerted. Premeditated choice is different from desire—from passion—from wishing—and from opinion. Desire and passion are common to animals, who are nevertheless incapable of *deliberate preference*. The incontinent man acts from desire, but not from deliberate preference : the continent man acts from deliberate preference, but not from desire. Nor is premeditated choice the same as wishing : for we often wish for what is notoriously impracticable or unattainable, but we do not deliberately prefer any such thing: moreover we *wish* for the end, but we *deliberately choose* the means conducting to the end. We wish to be happy : but it cannot with propriety be said that we deliberately choose to be happy. Deliberate choice has reference to what it is or seems in our own power to achieve.

Again, deliberate choice is not to be regarded as a simple modification of opinion. Opinion extends to every thing: deliberate choice belongs exclusively to matters within our grasp. Opinion is either true or false: deliberate choice is either good or evil. We are good or bad, according to the turn which our deliberate choice takes : not according to our opinions. We deliberately choose to seek something or to avoid something, and our choice is praised when it falls upon what is proper: the points upon which we form an opinion are, what such or such a thing is, whom it will benefit, and how : and our opinion is praised when it happens to be true. It often occurs, too, that men who form the truest opinions are not the best in their deliberate preferences. Opinion may precede or accompany every deliberate choice, but still the latter is something distinct in itself. It is in fact a determination of the will, preceded by deliberate counsel, and thus including or presupposing the employment of reason (ii. 2). It is an appetency, determined by previous counsel, of some matter within our means, either really or seemingly, to accomplish—βουλευτικὴ ὄρεξις τῶν ἐφ' ἡμῖν (ii. 3).

It seems from the language of Aristotle that the various explanations of Προαίρεσις which he has canvassed and shewn to be inadmissible, had all been advanced by various contemporary philosophers.

Προαίρεσις, or *deliberate preference,* includes the idea of *deliberation.* A reasonable man does not deliberate upon all matters—he does not deliberate respecting mathematical or physical truths, or respecting natural events altogether out of his reach, or respecting matters of pure accident, or even respecting matters of human design carried on by distant foreign nations. He only deliberates respecting matters which are more or less within his own agency and controul : respecting matters which are not certain, but of doubtful issue. He does not deliberate about the end, but about the means towards the end : the end itself is commonly assumed, just as the physician assumes the necessity of establishing good health and the orator that of persuading his hearers. If there be more than one way of accomplishing the end, he deliberates by

which out of these several means he can achieve it
best and most easily : proceeding from the end itself
first to the proximate cause of that end, then to the
cause immediately preceding that cause, and so back-
wards until he arrives at the primary cause, which is
either an action of his own, within his own means,
or something requiring implements and assistance
beyond his power to procure. This is a process of
analysis, similar to that which is pursued by geometri-
cians in seeking the way of solving a problem : they
assume the figure with the required conditions to be
constructed; they then take it to pieces, following back
the consequences of each separate condition which it
has been assumed to possess. If by this way of
proceeding they arrive at some known truth, their
problem is solved : if they arrive at some known
untruth, the problem is insoluble. That step which
is last arrived at in the analysis, is the first in the
order of production (iii. 3). When a man in carry-
ing back mentally this deliberative analysis arrives
at something manifestly impracticable, he desists
from farther deliberation : if he arrives at something
within his power to perform, he begins action
accordingly. The subject of *deliberation*, and the
subject of *deliberate preference*, are the same, but the
latter represents the process as accomplished and the
result of deliberation decided.

We take counsel and deliberation (as has been

said), not about the end, but about the means or the best means towards the end assumed. We *wish for the end* (ἡ βούλησις τοῦ τέλους ἐστι—iii. 4). Our wish is for good, real or apparent: whether for the one or the other, is a disputed question. Speaking generally, and without reference to peculiar idiosyncrasies, the real good or *the good* is the object of human wishes: speaking with reference to any particular individual, it is his own supposed or apparent good. On this matter, the virtuous man is the proper judge and standard of reference: that which is really good appears good to him. Each particular disposition has its own peculiar sentiment both of what is honourable and of what is agreeable (iii. 4): the principal excellence of the virtuous man is, that he in every variety of circumstances perceives what is truly and genuinely good; whereas to most men, pleasure proves a deception, and appears to be good, not being so in reality.

Both virtue and vice consist in *deliberate preference*, of one or of another course of action. Both therefore are voluntary and in our own power: both equally so. It is not possible to refer virtuous conduct or vicious conduct to any other beginning except to ourselves: the man is the cause of his own actions, as he is the father of his own children. It is upon this assumption that all legal reward and punishment is founded: it is intended for purposes of encouragement and prevention, but it would be absurd to think either of encouraging or preventing what is involuntary, such as the appetite of hunger and thirst. A man is punished for ignorance, when he is himself the cause of his own ignorance, or when by reasonable pains he might have acquired the requisite knowledge. Every man above the limit of absolute fatuity (κομιδῇ ἀναισθήτου) must know that any constant repetition of acts tends to form a habit: if then by repetition of acts he allows himself to form a bad habit, it is his own fault. When once the bad habit is formed, it is true that he cannot at once get rid of it : but the formation of such a habit originally was not the less imputable to himself (iii. 5). Defects of body also which we bring upon ourselves by our own negligence or intemperance, bring upon us censure : if they are constitutional and unavoidable, we are pitied for them. Some persons seem to have contended at that time, that no man could justly be made responsible for his bad conduct: because (they said) the end which he proposed to himself was good or bad according to his natural disposition, not according to any selection of his own. Aristotle seems to be somewhat perplexed by this argument: nevertheless he maintains, that whatever influence we may allow to original and uncontrollable nature, still the formation of our habits is more or less under our own concurrent controul; and therefore the end which we propose to ourselves being dependent upon those habits, is also in part at least dependent upon ourselves (iii. 5)—our virtues and our vices are both voluntary.

The first five chapters of the third Book (in which Aristotle examines the nature of τὸ ἑκούσιον, τὸ ἀκούσιον, προαίρεσις, βούλησις, &c.) ought perhaps to constitute a Book by themselves. They are among the most valuable parts of the Ethics. He has now established certain points with regard to our virtues generally.

1. They are mediocrities (μεσότητες).

2. They are habits, generated by particular actions often repeated.

3. When generated, they have a specific influence of their own in facilitating the performance of actions of the same class.

4. They are in our own power originally, and voluntary.

5. They are under the direction of right reason.

It is to be observed that our actions are voluntary from the beginning to the end—the last of a number of repeated actions is no less voluntary than the first. But our habits are voluntary only at the beginning—they cease to be voluntary after a certain time—but the permanent effect left by each separate repetition of the action is inappreciable (iii. 5).

Aristotle then proceeds to an analysis of the separate virtues—Courage, Temperance, Liberality, Magnificence, Magnanimity, Gentleness, Frankness, Simplicity, Elegant playfulness, Justice, Equity, &c. He endeavours to shew that each of these is a certain mediocrity—excess lying on one side of it, defect on the other.

There are various passages of Aristotle which appear almost identical with the moral doctrine subsequently maintained by the Stoic school: for example—iii. 6—" In like manner he ought not to fear penury, nor sickness, nor in any way such things as arise not from moral baseness nor are dependent on himself."

The courageous man is afraid of things such as it befits a man to fear, but of no others : and even these he will make head against on proper occasions, when reason commands and for the sake of *honour*, which is the end of virtue (iii. 7). To fear nothing, or too little, is rashness or insanity: to fear too much, is timidity : the courageous man is the mean between the two, who fears what he ought, when he ought, as he ought, and with the right views and purposes (*ib.*). The μοιχὸs (adulterer) exposes himself often to great dangers for the purpose of gratifying his passion : but Aristotle does not hold this to be courage. Neither does he thus denominate men who affront danger from passion, or from the thirst of revenge, or from a sanguine temperament—there must be deliberate preference and a proper motive, to constitute courage—the motive of honour (iii. 8).

The end of courage (says Aristotle) is in itself pleasant, but it is put out of sight by the circumstances around it: just as the prize for which the pugilist contends is in itself pleasurable, but being of small moment and encompassed with painful accessories, it appears to carry with it no pleasure whatever. Fatigue, and wounds and death are painful to the courageous man—death is indeed more painful to him, inasmuch as his life is of more value: but still he voluntarily and knowingly affronts these pains for the sake of honour.

This is painful: " but pleasure is not to be anticipated in the exercise of all the different virtues, except in so far as the attainment of the end is concerned" (iii. 9).

(This is perfectly true : but it contradicts decidedly the remark which Aristotle had made before in his first Book (i. 8) respecting the inherent pleasure of virtuous agency.)

Courage and Temperance are the virtues of the instincts (τῶν ἀλόγων μερῶν—iii. 10). Temperance is the observance of a rational medium with respect to the pleasures of eating, drinking, and sex. Aristotle seems to be inconsistent when he makes it to belong to those pleasures in which animals generally

partake (iii. 10) ; for other animals do not relish
intoxicating liquors: unless indeed these are considered as ranking under *drink* generally.   The
temperate man desires these pleasures as he ought,
when he ought, within the limits of what is honourable, and having a proper reference to the amount
of his own pecuniary means: just as right reason
prescribes (iii. 11).   To pursue them more, is excess :
to pursue them less, is defect.   There is however, in
estimating excess and defect, a certain tacit reference
to the average dispositions of the many.

"Wherefore the desires of the temperate man
ought to harmonize with reason ; for the aim of both
is the honourable.   And the temperate man desires
what he ought, and as he ought, and when : and this
too is the order of reason " (iii. 12).

All virtuous acts are to be *on account of the honourable*—thus Aristòtle says that the donations of the
ἄσωτος (prodigal) are not to be called liberal—
"Neither are their gifts liberal, for they are not
honourable, nor on account of this, nor as they
ought to be " (iv. 1).   Again about the μεγα-
λοπρεπὴς or *magnificent* man — "Now the magnificent man will expend such things on account
of the honourable; for this is a condition shared
in by all the virtues: and still he will do so
pleasantly and lavishly " (iv. 2).   On the contrary,
the βάναυσος or *vulgar* man, who differs from the

magnificent man in the way of ὑπερβολὴ or *excess*, is said to spend—" Not for the sake of the honourable, but for the purpose of making. a display of his wealth " (iv. 2).

With respect to those epithets which imply praise or blame, there is always a tacit comparison with some assumed standard. Thus with regard to the φιλότιμος (lover of honour), Aristotle observes— " It is evident that, as the term ' lover of such and such things ' is used in various senses, we do not always apply ' lover of honour' to express the same thing ; but when we praise, we praise that ambition which is more than most men's, and blame that which is greater than it ought to be " (iv. 4).

In the fifth Book, Aristotle proceeds to explain wherein consist *Justice* and *Injustice*.

These words are used in two senses—a larger sense and a narrower sense.

In the larger sense, *just behaviour* is equivalent to the observance of law, generally : unjust behaviour is equivalent to the violation of law generally. But the law either actually does command, or may be understood to command, that we should perform towards others the acts belonging to each separate head of virtue : it either actually prohibits, or may be understood to prohibit, us from performing towards others any of the acts belonging to each separate head of vice. In this larger sense, therefore, *justice* is synonymous generally with perfect virtue—*injustice*, with perfect wickedness : there is only this difference, that *just* or *unjust* are expressions applied to behaviour in so far as it affects other persons besides the agent : whereas *virtuous* or *wicked* are expressions applied simply to the agent without connoting any such ulterior reference to other persons. *Just* or *unjust*, is necessarily towards somebody else : and this reference is implied distinctly in the term. Virtuous and vicious do not in the force of the term connote any such relations, but are employed with reference to the agent simply—" This justice then is perfect virtue ; yet not absolutely, but with reference to one's neighbour.—In one sense we call those things *just* that are productive and preservative of happiness and its parts to the political communion " (v. 1).

Justice in this sense, is the very fulness of virtue, because it denotes the actual exercise of virtuous behaviour towards others : " there are many who behave virtuously in regard to their own personal affairs, but who are incapable of doing so in what regards others " (*ib.*). For this reason, justice has been called by some *the good of another and not our own*—justice alone of all the virtues, because it necessarily has reference to another : the just man does what is for the interest of some one else, either the magistrate, or the community (v. 1).

Justice in the narrower sense, is that mode of

behaviour whereby a man, in his dealings with others, aims at taking to himself his fair share and no more of the common objects of desire: and willingly consents to endure his fair share of the common hardships. *Injustice* is the opposite—that by which a man tries to appropriate more than his fair share of the objects of desire, while he tries to escape his fair share of the objects of aversion. To aim at this unfair distribution of the benefits of the society, either in one's own favour or in favour of any one else, is *injustice in the narrow sense* (v. 2).

Justice in this narrower sense is divided into two branches — 1. Distributive Justice.   2. Corrective Justice.

Distributive Justice has reference to those occasions on which positive benefits are to be distributed among the members of the community, wealth and honours, &c. (v. 2). In this case, the share of each citizen is to be a share not absolutely of equality, but one proportional to his personal worth (ἀξίαν): and it is in the estimation of this personal worth that quarrels and dissension arise.

Corrective Justice has reference to the individual dealings, or individual behaviour, between man and man: either to the dealings implying mutual consent and contract, as purchase, sale, loan, hire, suretyship, deposit, &c.: or such as imply no such mutual consent,—such as are on the contrary proceedings either by fraud or by force—as theft, adultery, perjury, poisoning, assassination, robbery, beating, mutilation, murder, defamation, &c.

In regard to transactions of this nature, the citizens are considered as being all upon a par—no account is taken of the difference between them in point of individual worth.   Each man is considered as en-titled to an equal share of good and evil: and if in any dealings between man and man, one man shall attempt to increase his own share of good or to diminish his own share of evil at the expense of another man, corrective justice will interpose and re-establish the equality thus improperly disturbed. He who has been made to lose or to suffer unduly, must be compensated and replaced in his former position: he who has gained unduly, must be mulcted or made to suffer, so as to be thrown back to the point from which he started.   The judge, who repre-sents this *corrective justice*, is a kind of mediator, and the point which he seeks to attain in directing re-dress, is *the middle point between gain and loss*—so that neither shall the aggressive party be a gainer, nor the suffering party a loser—"So that justice is a mean between a sort of gain and loss in voluntary things,—it is the having the same after as before" (v. 4).   Aristotle admits that the words *gain* and *loss* are not strictly applicable to many of the trans-actions which come within the scope of interference from *corrective justice*—that they properly belong to voluntary contracts, and are strained in order to apply them to acts of aggression, &c. (*ib.*).

The Pythagoreians held the doctrine that justice universally speaking consisted in simple retaliation—in rendering to another the precise dealing which that other had first given. This definition will not suit either for distributive justice or corrective justice : the treatment so prescribed would be sometimes more, sometimes less, than justice : not to mention that acts deserve to be treated differently according as they are intentional or unintentional. But the doctrine is to a certain extent true in regard to the dealings between man and man (ἐν ταῖς ἀλλακτικαῖς κοινωνίαις)—if it be applied in the way of general analogy and not with any regard to exact similarity—it is of importance that the man who has been well treated, and the man who has been ill-treated, should each show his sense of the proceeding by returning the like usage : " for by proportionate requital the State is held together " (v. 5). The whole business of exchange and barter, of division of labour and occupation,—the co-existence of those distinct and heterogeneous ingredients which are requisite to constitute the political communion—the supply of the most essential wants of the citizens—is all founded upon the continuance and the expectation of this assured requital for acts done. Money is introduced as an indispensable instrument for facilitating this constant traffic: it affords a common measure for estimating the value of every service—" And thus if there were no possibility of retaliation, there would be no communion " (v. 5).

Justice is thus a mediocrity—or consists in a just medium—between two extremes, but not in the same way as the other virtues. The just man is one who awards both to himself and to every one else the proper and rightful share both of benefit and burthen. Injustice, on the contrary, consists in the excess or defect which lie on one side or the other of this medium point (v. 5).

Distributive justice is said by Aristotle to deal with individuals according to geometrical ratio; *corrective justice*, according to arithmetical proportion. *Justice*, strictly and properly so called, is *political justice*: that reciprocity of right and obligation which prevails between free and equal citizens in a community, or between citizens who, if not positively equal, yet stand in an assured and definite ratio one to the other (v. 6). This relation is defined and maintained by law, and by judges and magistrates to administer the law. Political justice implies a state of law—a community of persons qualified by nature to obey and sustain the law—and a definite arrangement between the citizens in respect to the alternation of command and obedience—" For this is, as we have said ($\hat{\tilde{\eta}}\nu$), according to law, and among those who can naturally have law; those, namely, as we have said (ἦσαν), who have an equality of ruling and being ruled." As the law arises out of the necessity of preventing injustice, or of hindering any individual from appropriating more than his fair share of good things, so it is felt that any person invested with sovereign authority may and will commit this injustice. Reason therefore is understood to hold the sovereign authority, and the archon acts only as the guardian of the reciprocal rights and obligations—of the constitutional equality—between the various citizens: undertaking a troublesome duty and paid for his trouble by honour and respect (v. 6).

The relation which subsists between master and slave, or father and son, is not properly speaking that of justice, though it is somewhat analogous. Both the slave, and the non-adult son; are as it were parts of the master and father: there can therefore be no injustice on his part towards them, since no one deliberately intends to hurt a part of himself. Between husband and wife there subsists a sort of justice—*household justice* (τὸ οἰκονομικὸν δίκαιον)—but this too is different from political justice (v. 6).

Political justice is in part *natural*—in part *conventional*. That which is *natural* is everywhere the same: that which is *conventional* is different in different countries, and takes its origin altogether from positive and special institution. Some persons think that *all* political justice is thus conventional, and none natural: because they see that rights and obligations (τὰ δίκαια) are everywhere changeable, and nowhere exhibit that permanence and invariability which mark the properties of natural objects. "This is true to a certain extent, but not wholly true: probably among the Gods it is not true at all: but with us that which is natural is in part variable, though not in every case: yet there is a real distinction between what is natural and what is not natural. Both natural justice and conventional justice, are thus alike contingent and variable; but there is a clear mode of distinguishing between the two, applicable not only to the case of justice but to other cases in which the like distinction is to be taken. For by nature the right hand is the stronger: but nevertheless it may happen that there are ambidextrous men.—And in like manner those rules of justice which are not natural, but of human establishment, are not the same everywhere: nor indeed does the same mode of government prevail everywhere, though there is but one mode of government which is everywhere agreeable to nature—the best of all" (v. 7).

(The commentary of Andronicus upon this passage is clearer and more instructive than the passage of Aristotle itself: and it is remarkable as a distinct announcement of the principle of utility. "Since both natural justice, and conventional justice, are changeable, in the way just stated, how are we to distinguish the one of these fluctuating institutions from the other? The distinction is plain. Each special precept of justice is to be examined on its own ground, to ascertain whether it be for the advantage of all that it should be maintained unaltered, or whether the subversion of it would occasion mischief. If this be found to be the fact, the precept in question belongs to natural justice: if it be otherwise, to conventional justice" (Andronic. Rh. v. c. 10).

The just, and the unjust, being thus defined, a man who does, willingly and knowingly, either the one or the other, acts justly or unjustly: if he does it unwillingly or unknowingly, he neither acts justly nor unjustly, except by accident—that is, he does what is not essentially and in its own nature unjust, but is only so by accident (v. 8). Injustice will thus have been done, but no unjust act will have been committed, if the act be done involuntarily. The man who restores a deposit unwillingly and from fear of danger to himself, does not act justly, though he does what by accident is just: the man who, anxious to restore the deposit, is prevented by positive superior force from doing so, does not act unjustly, although he does what by accident is unjust. When a man does mischief, it is either done contrary to all reasonable expectation, in such

manner that neither he nor any one else could
have anticipated from his act the mischief which
has actually ensued from it (παραλόγως), and in this
case it is a pure misfortune (ἀτύχημα): or he does it
without intention or foreknowledge, yet under circumstances in which mischief might have been foreseen, and ought to have been foreseen; in this case
it is a fault (ἁμάρτημα): or he does it intentionally
and with foreknowledge, yet without any previous
deliberation, through anger, or some violent momentary impulse; in this case it is an unjust act (ἀδί-
κημα), but the agent is not necessarily an *unjust or
wicked* man for having done it: or he does it with
intention and deliberate choice, and in this case he
is an unjust and wicked man.

The man who does a just thing, or an unjust thing,
is not necessarily a just or an unjust man. Whether
he be so or not, depends upon the state of his mind
and intention at the time (v. 8).

Equity, τὸ ἐπιεικὲς, is not at variance with justice,
but is an improvement upon justice. It is a correc-
tion and supplement to the inevitable imperfections
in the definitions of legal justice. The law wishes
to comprehend all cases, but fails in doing so: the
words of its enactment do not fully and exactly
express its real intentions, but either something
more or something less. When the lawgiver speaks
in general terms, a particular case may happen

which falls within the rule as he lays it down, but which he would not have wished to comprehend if he had known how to avoid it. It is then becoming conduct in the individual to whose advantage the law in this special case turns, that he should refrain from profiting by his position, and that he should act as the legislator himself would wish, if consulted on the special case. The general rules laid down by the legislator are of necessity more or less defective : in fact, the only reason why every thing is not determined by law, is, that there are some matters respecting which it is impossible to frame a law (v. 10). Such is the conduct of the equitable man— "the man who refrains from pushing his legal rights to the extreme, to the injury of others, but who foregoes the advantage of his position, although the law is in his favour" (ὁ μὴ ἀκριβοδίκαιος ἐπὶ χεῖρον, ἀλλ᾽ ἐλαττωτικὸς, καίπερ ἔχων τὸν νόμον βοηθόν).

A man may hurt himself, but he cannot act unjustly towards himself. No injustice can be done to a man except against his own consent. Suicide is by implication forbidden by the law: to commit suicide is wrong, because a man in so doing acts unjustly towards the city, not towards himself, which is impossible (v. 11).

To act unjustly—and to be the object of unjust dealing by others—are both bad: but which is the

worst? It is the least of the two evils to be the
object of unjust dealing by others. Both are bad,
because in the one case a man gets more than his
share, in the other less than his share: in both cases
the just medium is departed from. To act unjustly
is blameable, and implies wickedness: to be the object
of unjust dealing by others is not blameable, and
implies no wickedness: the latter is therefore in
itself the least evil, although by accident it may
perhaps turn out to be the greater evil of the two.
In the same manner a pleurisy is in itself a greater
evil than a trip and a stumble: but by accident it
may turn out that the latter is the greater evil of the
two, if it should occur at the moment when a man is
running away from the enemy, so as to cause his
being taken prisoner and slain.

The question here raised by Aristotle—which is
the greater evil—to act unjustly or to be the object
of unjust dealing—had been before raised by Plato
in the Gorgias. Aristotle follows out his theory
about virtue, whereby he makes it consist in the
observance of a medium point. The man that acts
unjustly sins on one side of this point, the object of
unjust dealing misses it on the other side: the one is
comparable to a man who eats or works too much for
his health, the other to a man who eats or works too
little. The question is one which could hardly
arise, according to the view taken by modern ethical

writers of the principles of moral science. The two things compared are not in point of fact commensurable. Looking at the question from the point of view of the moralist, the person injured has incurred no moral guilt, but has suffered more or less of misfortune : the unjust agent on the contrary has suffered no misfortune—perhaps he has reaped benefit—but at any rate he has incurred moral guilt. Society on the whole is a decided loser by the act : but the wrong done implies the suffering inflicted : the act is considered and called *wrong* because it does inflict suffering, and for no other reason. It seems an inadmissible question therefore, to ask which of the two is the greater evil—the suffering undergone by A—or the wrong by which B occasioned that suffering : at least so far as society is concerned.

But the ancient moralists, in instituting this comparison, seem to have looked, not at society, but at the two individuals—the wrong doer and the wrong sufferer—and to have looked at them too from a point of view of their own. If we take the feelings of these two parties themselves as the standard by which to judge, the sentence must be obviously contrary to the opinion delivered by Aristotle : the sufferer, according to his own feeling, is worse off than he was before : the doer is better off. And it is for this reason that the act forms a proper ground for judicial punishment or redress. But the moralist estimates the condition of the two men by a standard of his own, not by the feelings which they themselves entertain. He decides for himself that a virtuous frame of mind is the primary and essential ingredient of individual happiness—a wicked frame of mind the grand source of misery: and by this test he tries the comparative happiness of every man. The man who manifests evidence of a guilty frame of mind is decidedly worse off than he who has only suffered an unmerited misfortune.

ESSAY VI.

THE POLITICS OF ARISTOTLE.

THE POLITICS OF ARISTOTLE.

THE scheme of government proposed by Aristotle, in the two last books of his Politics, as representing his own ideas of something like perfection, is evidently founded upon the Republic of Plato: from whom he differs in the important circumstance of not admitting either community of property or community of wives and children.

Each of these philosophers recognises one separate class of inhabitants, relieved from all private toil and all money-getting employments, and constituting exclusively the citizens of the commonwealth. This small class is in effect *the city—the commonwealth :* the remaining inhabitants are not a part of the commonwealth, they are only appendages to it—indispensable indeed, but still appendages, in the same manner as slaves or cattle (vii. 8). In the Republic of Plato this narrow aristocracy are not allowed to possess private property or separate families, but form one inseparable brotherhood. In the scheme of Aristotle, this aristocracy form a distinct caste of private families each with its separate property.

The whole territory of the State belongs to them,
and is tilled by dependent cultivators, by whom the
produce is made over and apportioned under certain
restrictions.   A certain section of the territory is
understood to be the common property of the body
of citizens (*i.e.* of the aristocracy), and the produce
of it is handed over by the cultivators into a common
stock, partly to supply the public tables at which all
the citizens with their wives and families are sub-
sisted, partly to defray the cost of religious solem-
nities. The remaining portion of the territory is
possessed in separate properties by individual citizens,
who consume the produce as they please (vii. 9):
each citizen having two distinct lots of land assigned
to him, one near the outskirts of the territory, the
other near the centre. This latter regulation also
had been adopted by Plato in the treatise de Legibus,
and it is surprising to observe that Aristotle himself
had censured it, in his criticisms on that treatise, as
incompatible with a judicious and careful economy
(ii. 3. 8). The syssitia or public tables are also
adopted by Plato, in conformity with the institutions
actually existing in his time in Crete and elsewhere.

The dependent cultivators, in Aristotle's scheme,
ought to be slaves, not united together by any bond
of common language or common country (vii. 9, 9):
if this cannot be, they ought to be a race of subdued
foreigners, degraded into periœci, deprived of all use

of arms, and confined to the task of labouring in the field. Those slaves who till the common land are to be considered as the property of the collective body of citizens : the slaves on land belonging to individual citizens, are the property of those citizens.

When we consider the scanty proportion of inhabitants whom Aristotle and Plato include in the benefits of their community, it will at once appear how amazingly their task as political theorists is simplified. Their commonwealth is really an aristocracy on a very narrow scale. The great mass of the inhabitants are thrust out altogether from all security and good government, and are placed without reserve at the disposal of the small body of armed citizens.

There is but one precaution on which Aristotle and Plato rely for ensuring good treatment from the citizens towards their inferiors : and that is, the finished and elaborate education which the citizens are to receive. Men so educated, according to these philosophers, will behave as perfectly in the relation of superior to inferior, as in that of equal to equal— of citizen to citizen.

This supposition would doubtless prove true, to a certain extent, though far short of that extent which would be requisite to assure the complete comfort of the inferior. But even if it were true to the fullest extent, it would be far from satisfying the demands

of a benevolent theorist.   For though the inferior
should meet with kindness and protection from his
superior, still his mind must be kept in a degradation
suitable to his position.   He must be deprived of all
moral and intellectual culture: he must be prevented
from imbibing any ideas of his own dignity: he
must be content to receive whatever is awarded, to
endure whatever treatment is vouchsafed, without
for an instant imagining that he has a right to
benefits or that suffering is wrongfully inflicted upon
him.   Both Plato and Aristotle acknowledge the inevitable depravation and moral abasement of all the
inhabitants excepting their favoured class.   Neither
of them seems solicitous either to disguise or to
mitigate it.

But if they are thus indifferent about the moral
condition of the mass, they are in the highest degree
exact and careful respecting that of their select
citizens.   This is their grand and primary object,
towards which the whole force of their intellect, and
the full fertility of their ingenious imagination, is
directed.   Their plans of education are most elaborate and comprehensive: aiming at every branch of
moral and intellectual improvement, and seeking to
raise the whole man to a state of perfection, both
physical and mental.   You would imagine that they
were framing a scheme of public education, not a
political constitution: so wholly are their thoughts

engrossed with the training and culture of their citizens. It is in this respect that their ideas are truly instructive.

Viewed with reference to the general body of inhabitants in a State, nothing can be more defective than the plans of both these great philosophers. Assuming that their objects were completely attained, the mass of the people would receive nothing more than that degree of physical comfort and mild usage which can be made to consist with subjection and with the extortion of compulsory labour.

Viewed with reference to the special class recognised as citizens, the plans of both are to a high degree admirable. A better provision is made for the virtue as well as for the happiness of this particular class than has ever been devised by any other political projector. The intimate manner in which Aristotle connects virtue with happiness, is above all remarkable. He in fact defines happiness to consist in *the active exertion and perfected habit of virtue* (ἀρετῆς ἐνέργεια καὶ χρῆσίς τις τέλειος—vi. 9. 3.) : and it is upon this disposition that he founds the necessity of excluding the mass of inhabitants from the citizenship. For the purpose to be accomplished by the political union, is, the assuring of happiness to every individual citizen, which is to be effected by implanting habits of virtue in every citizen. Whoever therefore is incapable of acquiring habits of virtue, is disqualified from becoming a citizen. But every man whose life is spent in laborious avocations, whether of husbandry, of trade, or of manufacture, becomes thereby incapable of acquiring habits of virtue, and cannot therefore be admitted to the citizenship. No man can be capable of the requisite mental culture and tuition, who is not exempted from the necessity of toil, enabled to devote his whole time to the acquisition of virtuous habits, and sub-jected from his infancy to a severe and systematic training. The exclusion of the bulk of the people from civil rights is thus founded, in the mind of Aristotle, on the lofty idea which he forms of indivi-dual human perfection, which he conceives to be absolutely unattainable unless it be made the sole object of a man's life. But then he takes especial care that the education of his citizens shall be really such as to compel them to acquire that virtue on which alone their pre-eminence is built. If he ex-empts them from manual or money-getting labours, he imposes upon them an endless series of painful restraints and vexatious duties for the purpose of forming and maintaining their perfection of character. He allows no luxury or self-indulgence, no mis-appropriation of time, no ostentatious display of wealth or station. The life of his select citizens would be such as to provoke little envy or jealousy, among men of the ordinary stamp. Its hard work and its strict discipline would appear repulsive rather than inviting : and the pre-eminence of strong and able men, submitting to such continued schooling, would appear well deserved and hardly earned.

Oligarchical reasoners in modern times employ the bad part of Aristotle's principle without the good. They represent the rich and great as alone capable of reaching a degree of virtue consistent with the full enjoyment of political privileges : but then they take no precautions, as Aristotle does, that the men so preferred shall really answer to this exalted character. They leave the rich and great to their own self-indulgence and indolent propensities, without training them by any systematic process to habits of superior virtue. So that the select citizens on this plan are at the least no better, if indeed they are not worse, than the remaining community, while their unbounded indulgences excite either undue envy or undue admiration, among the excluded multitude. The select citizens of Aristotle are both better and wiser than the rest of their community : while they are at the same time so hemmed in and circumscribed by severe regulations, that nothing except the perfection of their character can appear worthy either of envy or admiration. Though therefore these oligarchical reasoners concur with Aristotle in sacrificing the bulk of the community to the pre-eminence of a narrow class, they fail of accomplishing the end

for which alone he pretends to justify such a sacrifice
—the formation of a few citizens of complete and
unrivalled virtue.

The arrangements made by Aristotle for the good
government of his aristocratical citizens among themselves, are founded upon principles of the most
perfect equality.   He would have them only limited
in number, for in his opinion, personal and familiar
acquaintance among them all is essentially requisite
to good government (vii. 4. 7).   The principal offices
of the State are all to be held by the aged citizens :
the military duties are to be fulfilled by the younger
citizens.   The city altogether, with the territory
appertaining to it, must be large enough to be
αὐτάρκης : but it must not be so extensive as to
destroy personal intimacy among the citizens.   A
very large body are, in Aristotle's view, incapable of
discipline or regularity.

To produce a virtuous citizen, *nature, habit,* and
reason must coincide.   They ought to be endued with
virtues qualifying them both for occupation and for
leisure : with courage, self-denial (καρτερία), and forti-
tude, to maintain their independence : with justice
and temperance, to restrain them from abusing the
means of enjoyment provided for them : and with
philosophy or the love of contemplative wisdom and
science, in order to banish ennui, and render the
hours of leisure agreeable to them (vii. 13. 17).

They are to be taught that their hours of leisure are of greater worth and dignity than their hours of occupation. Occupation is to be submitted to for the sake of the quiet enjoyment of leisure, just as war is made for the sake of procuring peace, and useful and necessary employments undertaken for the sake of those which are honourable (vii. 13. 8). Aristotle greatly censures (see vii. 2. 5) (as indeed Plato had done before him) the institutions of Lacedæmon, as being directed exclusively to create excellent warriors, and to enable the nation to rule over foreigners. This (he says) is not only not the right end, but is an end absolutely pernicious and culpable. To maintain a forcible sovereignty over free and equal foreigners, is unjust and immoral : and if the minds of the citizens be corrupted with this collective ambition and love of power, it is probable that some individual citizen, taught by the education of the State to consider power as the first of all earthly ends, will find an opportunity to aggrandize himself by force or fraud, and to establish a tyranny over his countrymen themselves (viii. 13. 13). The Lacedæ-monians conducted themselves well and flourished under their institutions, so long as they were carry-ing on war for the enlargement of their dominion : but they were incapable of tasting or profiting by peace : they were not educated by their legislator so as to be able to turn leisure to account (αἴτιος δ' ὁ νομοθέτης, οὐ παιδεύσας δύνασθαι σχολάζειν—vii. 13. 15).

The education of the citizen is to commence with the body : next the irrational portion of the soul is to be brought under discipline—that is, the will and the appetites, the concupiscent and irascible passions : thirdly, the rational portion of the soul is to be cultivated and developed.   The habitual desires are to be so moulded and tutored as to prepare them for the sovereignty of reason, when the time shall arrive for bringing reason into action (vii. 13. 23).   They are to learn nothing until five years old (vii. 15. 4), their diversions are to be carefully prepared and presented to them, consisting generally of a mimicry of subsequent serious occupations (vii. 15. 15) : and all the fables and tales which they hear recited are to be such as to pave the way for moral discipline (ib.) ; all under the superintendence of the Pædonom.   No obscene or licentious talk is to be tolerated in the city (vii. 15. 7), nor any indecent painting or statue, except in the temples of some particular Deities. No youth is permitted to witness the recitation either of iambics or of comedy (vii. 15. 9), until he attains the age which qualifies him to sit at the public tables.   Immense stress is laid by the philosopher on the turn of ideas to which the tender minds of youth become accustomed, and on the earliest combinations of sounds or of visible objects which meet their senses

(vii. 15. 10).   Πρὸς πάσας δυνάμεις καὶ τέχνας ἐστιν ἃ
δεῖ προπαιδεύεσθαι καὶ προεθίζεσθαι πρὸς τὰς ἑκάστων
ἐργασίας, ὥστε δῆλον ὅτι καὶ πρὸς τὰς τῆς ἀρετῆς
πράξεις (viii. 1. 2).

All the citizens in Aristotle's republic are to be
educated according to one common system : each
being regarded as belonging to the commonwealth
more than to his own parents.   This was the practice
at Lacedæmon, and Aristotle greatly eulogizes it
(viii. 1. 3).

Aristotle does not approve of extreme and violent
bodily training, such as would bring the body into
the condition of an athlete : nor does he even
sanction the gymnastic labours imposed by the
Lacedæmonian system, which had the effect of
rendering the Spartans "brutal of soul," for the
purpose of exalting their courage (οἱ Λάκωνες—
θηριώδεις ἀπεργάζονται τοῖς πόνοις, ὡς τοῦτο μάλιστα
πρὸς ἀνδρείαν σύμφερον).   He remarks, first, that
courage is not the single or exclusive end to be aimed
at in a civil education : next, that a savage and brutal
soul is less compatible with exalted courage than a
gentle soul, trained so as to be exquisitely sensible to
the feelings of shame and honour (viii. 3. 3–5).   The
most sanguinary and unfeeling among the barbarous
tribes, he remarks, were very far from being the
most courageous.   A man trained on the Lacedæmonian system, in bodily exercises alone, destitute

even of the most indispensable mental culture (see below), was a real βάναυσος—useful only for one branch of political duties, and even for that less useful than if he had been trained in a different manner.

Up to the age of 14, Aristotle prescribes (ἥβη means 14 years of age—see vii. 15. 11) that boys shall be trained in gentle and regular exercises, without any severe or forced labour. From 14 to 17 they are to be instructed in various branches of knowledge : after 17, they are to be put to harder bodily labour, and to be nourished with a special and peculiar diet (ἀναγκοφαγίαις). For how long this is to continue, is not stated. But Aristotle insists on the necessity of not giving them at the same time intellectual instruction and bodily training, for the one of these, he says, counteracts and frustrates the other (viii. 4. 2–3).

The Lacedæmonians made music no part of their education : Isocrat. Panathen. Or. xii. p. 375, B.; they did not even learn 'letters' (γράμματα), but they are said to have been good judges of music (viii. 4. 6). Aristotle himself however seems to think it next to impossible that men who have not learned music can be good judges (viii. 6. 1).

Aristotle admits that music may be usefully learnt as an innocent pleasure and relaxation : but he chiefly considers it as desirable on account of its

moral effects, on the dispositions and affections. A
right turn of the pleasurable and painful emotions is,
in his opinion, essential to virtue : particular strains
and particular rhythms are naturally associated with
particular dispositions of mind : by early teaching,
those strains and those rhythms which are associated
with temperate and laudable dispositions may be
made more agreeable to a youth than any others.
He will like best those which he hears earliest, and
which he finds universally commended and relished
by those about him.   A relish for the ὁμοιώματα of
virtuous dispositions will tend to increase in him the
love of virtue itself (viii. 6. 5–8).

Aristotle enjoins that the youth be taught to
execute music instrumentally and vocally, because it
is only in this way that they can acquire a good
taste or judgment in music : besides which, it is
necessary to furnish boys with some occupation, to
absorb their restless energies, and there is none more
suitable than music.   Some persons alleged that the
teaching music as a manual art was *banausic* and
degrading, lowering the citizen down to the station
of a hired professional singer.   Aristotle meets this
objection by providing that youths shall be instructed
in the musical art, but only with the view of correcting and cultivating their taste : they are to be forbidden from making any use of their musical acquisi-
tions, in riper years, in actual playing or singing

(viii. 6. 3). Aristotle observes, that music more difficult of execution had been recently introduced into the agones, and had found its way from the agones into the ordinary education. He decidedly disapproves and excludes it (viii. 6. 4). He forbids both the flute and the harp, and every other instrument requiring much art to play upon it : especially the flute, which he considers as not ethical, but orgiastical—calculated to excite violent and momentary emotions. The flute obtained a footing in Greece after the Persian invasion ; in Athens at that time it became especially fashionable : but was discontinued afterwards (Plutarch alleges, through the influence of Alcibiades).

The suggestions of Aristotle for the education of his citizen are far less copious and circumstantial than those of Plato in his Republic. He delivers no plan of study, no arrangement of sciences to be successively communicated, no reasons for preferring or rejecting. We do not know what it was precisely which Aristotle comprehended in the term ' philosophy,' intended by him to be taught to his citizens as an aid for the proper employment of their leisure. It must probably have included the moral, political, and metaphysical sciences, as they were then known—those sciences to which his own voluminous works relate.

By means of the public table, supplied from the produce of the public lands, Aristotle provides for the full subsistence of every citizen. Yet he is well aware that the citizens will be likely to increase in numbers too rapidly, and he suggests very efficient precautions against it. No child at all deformed or imperfect in frame is to be brought up: children beyond a convenient number, if born, are to be exposed: but should the law of the State forbid such a practice, care must be taken to forestall consciousness and life in them, and to prevent their birth by ἄμβλωσις (vii. 14. 10).

Aristotle establishes two *agora* in his city: one situated near to the harbour, adapted to the buying, selling, and storing of goods, under the surveillance of the agoranomus: the other called the *free agora*, situated in the upper parts of the city, set apart for the amusement and conversation of the citizens, and never defiled by the introduction of any commodities for sale. No artisan or husbandman is ever to enter the latter unless by special order from the authorities. The temples of the Gods, the residences of the various boards of government functionaries, the gymnasia of the older citizens, are all to be erected in this free agora (vii. 11). The Thessalian cities had an agora of this description where no traffic or common occupations were permitted.

The moral tendency of Aristotle's reflections is almost always useful and elevating. The intimate union which he formally recognises and perpetually proclaims between happiness and virtue, is salutary and instructive : and his ideas of what virtue is, are perfectly just, so far as relates to the conduct of his citizens towards each other : though they are miserably defective as regards obligation towards non-citizens. He always assigns the proper pre-eminence to wisdom and virtue : he never overvalues the advantages of riches, nor deems them entitled on their own account, to any reverence or submission : he allows no title to the obedience of mankind, except that which arises from superior power and disposition to serve them. Superior power and station, as he considers them, involve a series of troubles—some obligations which render them objects of desire only to men of virtue and beneficence. What is more rare and more creditable still, he treats all views of conquest and aggrandizement by a State as immoral and injurious, even to the conquerors themselves.

THE END.

LONDON: PRINTED BY WM. CLOWES AND SONS, STAMFORD STREET
AND CHARING CROSS.